simple knits with a twist

erika knight   photography by Graham Atkins Hughes

simple knits with a twist

UNIQUE PROJECTS FOR CREATIVE KNITTERS

STC CRAFT | A MELANIE FALICK BOOK | NEW YORK

This book is dedicated to all the anonymous people who have ever knitted, stitched, and created, going beyond function and practicality for the passion of their craft. They are, as always, my inspiration.

Published in 2004 by
STC Craft: A Melanie Falick Book
115 West 18th Street
New York, NY 10011
www.abramsbooks.com

Canadian Distribution:
Canada Manda Group
One Atlantic Avenue, Suite 105
Toronto, Ontario M6K 3E7

Simultaneously published in the United Kingdom
by Quadrille Publishing Limited 2004.

Library of Congess Cataloging-in-Publication
Data is available on record with the Library
of Congress.

ISBN 1-58479-361-9

The text of this book was composed in the
typeface Grotesque

Printed in China.
10 9 8 7 6 5 4 3

Stewart, Tabori & Chang is a subsidiary of

contents

techniques
and
textures

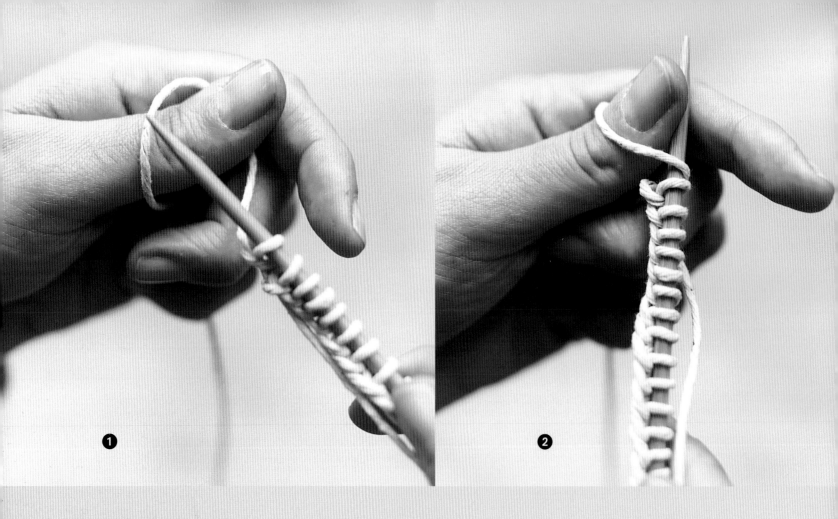

casting on

This is the very first thing you need to do in order to start knitting. Use this simple method of making the first stitches on a knitting needle using just a length of yarn and your thumb.

1 Measure a length of yarn that is long enough to create the number of stitches you are casting on (approximately 1 inch for each stitch in worsted-weight yarn, plus 2 inches for insurance). Hold the yarn at that point. Make a slipknot with the yarn at that point and place it on a knitting needle. * Hold the knitting needle with the loop of yarn in your right hand with the yarn from the ball. Take the loose end of the yarn in your left hand and form a loop around your left thumb.

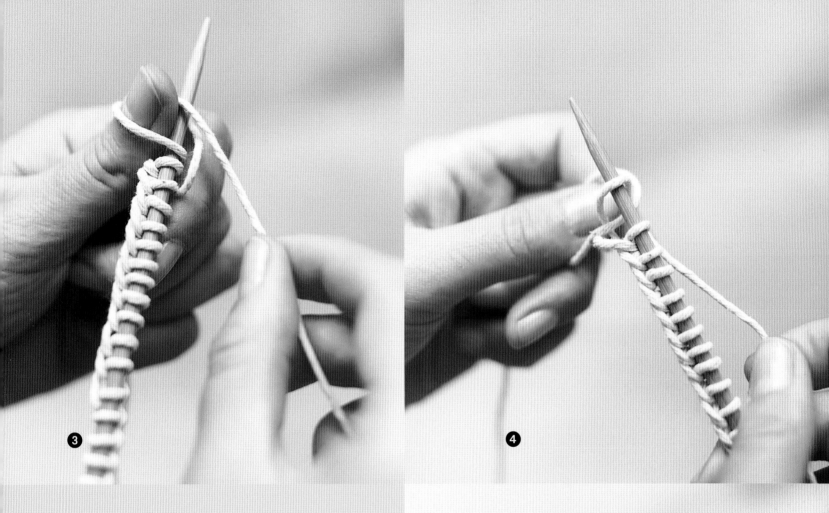

❸

❹

❷ Insert the point of the knitting needle
into the loop.

❸ With your right hand, wrap the yarn
from the ball over the point of the needle.

❹ Pull the needle under and through
the loop on your thumb.

❺ Slip the loop off your thumb and gently
tighten the stitch by pulling both strands.
Repeat these steps from * until you have
the required number of stitches.

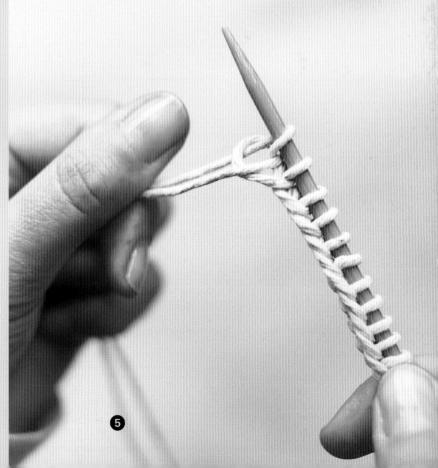

❺

binding off

This is usually the very last thing you need to do in order to finish knitting. It is the process that fixes a piece of knitting so that it does not unravel once taken off the needles.

1 At the beginning of your final row, knit the first two stitches as usual.

2 Insert the point of the left-hand needle into the center of the first knitted stitch on the right-hand needle.

3 Lift the first knitted stitch from the right-hand needle over the second knitted stitch on the right-hand needle.

4 Now remove the left-hand needle so only one knitted stitch remains on the right-hand

needle. Knit the next stitch on the left-hand needle, so there are two knitted stitches on the right-hand needle again. (See ❶.) Repeat these steps, making sure there are never more than two knitted stitches on the right-hand needle. ❺ Work until one stitch remains. Cut the working yarn. Pass the end of the yarn through the last loop. Remove the needle and pull on the end of the yarn to tighten.

knit stitch

After casting on the appropriate number of stitches, as shown on page 8, you can begin to knit your first row. Each stitch is made by the simple four-step process shown here. Each row is completed by repeating this process until all the stitches on the left-hand needle have been transferred to the right-hand needle. Once you have completed each row, transfer the needle holding the worked stitches to your left hand and begin again. Another row of knit stitches will create a fabric known as garter stitch (see page 22).

❶ Hold the needle with the cast-on stitches in your left hand. Holding the other needle in your right hand, insert the point of the right-hand needle into the first stitch on the

left-hand needle. Pass the needle under the loop facing you and up into the center of the stitch so the needles form an X shape, with the left-hand needle in front of the right-hand needle.

❷ Holding the working yarn in your right hand, and at the back of the work, wrap the yarn over the point of the right-hand needle to make a loop.

❸ Slide the right-hand needle toward you, passing the point down and out of the center of the stitch on the left-hand needle to pull the loop under and through the first stitch on the left-hand needle.

❹ Slide the original stitch off the point of the left-hand needle, leaving the new stitch on the right-hand needle. You have now knitted one stitch to the right-hand needle.

purl stitch

This stitch is worked in much the same way as the knit stitch, simply in reverse. When working the knit stitch, the yarn is held at the back of the work, but with the purl stitch, the yarn is held at the front of the work. Again, the purl stitch is made by the simple four-step process shown here. Repeat the process until the row is complete, and all the stitches have been transferred to the right-hand needle. Transfer this needle to your left hand before beginning the next row. Stockinette stitch is made by working one row knit, one row purl throughout (see page 23). The simple knit stitch and purl stitch is all there is to know! Combining the knit stitch and the purl stitch provides the basis of all knitted fabrics.

① Hold the needle with the cast-on stitches in your left hand. Holding the other needle in your right hand, and with the working yarn at the front of the work, insert the point of the right-hand needle into the front of the first stitch on the left-hand needle. Pass the needle from left to right through the center of the first stitch.

② Holding the working yarn in your right hand, and at the front of the work, wrap the yarn over the point of the right-hand needle to make a loop.

③ Slide the right-hand needle back and out of the first stitch on the left-hand needle to pull the loop through the first stitch on the left-hand needle.

④ Slide the original stitch off the point of the left-hand needle, leaving the new stitch on the right-hand needle. You have now purled one stitch to the right-hand needle.

increasing

Adding stitches or taking away stitches—increasing or decreasing—will shape your knitting. There are several ways to increase, but the simplest method is to knit into the same stitch twice to make an additional stitch.

❶ Knit into the first stitch on the left-hand needle as usual, but do not slip the original stitch off of the left-hand needle yet.

❷ Instead, place the loop on the right-hand needle back onto the left-hand needle, effectively adding a new stitch to your knitting.

❸ Knit all the stitches in the usual way, including the new stitch just added.

3

If the increase is worked on a purl stitch, purl through the first stitch as usual, wrapping the yarn over the needle and pulling a new loop through, but leave the original stitch on the left-hand needle. Transfer your working yarn to the back of the work, then insert the right-hand needle into the back of the same stitch on your left-hand needle and purl it again. Now slip the original stitch off the left-hand needle, leaving two stitches instead of the usual one on the right-hand needle.

decreasing

The simplest method of taking away stitches, or decreasing, is to knit two stitches together. Knitting the stitches together through the back of the loops (as shown here), forms a left-slanting decrease, and knitting through the front a right-slanting one.

❶ Instead of inserting the right-hand needle into one stitch on the left-hand needle, insert it into the first two stitches at the same time.

❷ Holding the working yarn in your right hand, and at the back of the work, wrap the yarn over the point of the right-hand needle to make a loop.

❸ Slide the right-hand needle toward you, passing the point down and out of the center

of the two stitches on the left-hand needle to pull the loop through the stitches on the left-hand needle.

4 Slide the original stitches off the point of the left-hand needle in the usual way, making sure that you drop both stitches from the left-hand needle. There is only one stitch knitted to the right-hand needle instead of two.

Decreases can also be worked on the purl row. Insert the point of the right-hand needle into the first two stitches on the left-hand needle at the same time and purl in the usual way, making sure that you drop both stitches from the left-hand needle. There is one stitch purled to the right-hand needle.

yarn textures

Let texture be your inspiration to design and make individual yarns to meet your personal requirements. It is not always easy to locate the specific yarns depicted in pattern books, either your nearest craft store is not that accessible or they do not have the yarns you want in the right colors or textures. So, what better than to create your own yarns from readily available sources?

You can use any continuous length of yarn to knit with, so it is just a matter of looking at an unconventional material in a different way and asking yourself whether it will meet your needs. Leather, wire, fabric, twine, linen, tape, ribbon, felt, denim, and rags, as well as more conventional wools, cottons, and tweeds, each is an inspiration for a textile project.

stitch textures

The simplest of stitches can create the most effective textures. My favorite stitch is seed stitch as it creates a very firm fabric, which is especially good for home-decorating projects, with a very discrete self-color pattern. An interesting variation is to work it in one strand of black yarn together with a strand of white yarn (see page 25).

Classic stockinette stitch is great for cotton projects in particular. Alternatively, use the reverse side for more texture but less bulk than garter stitch, which is also easy to do and wonderfully textural.

Traditional Aran techniques look hugely professional; I like to create oversized cables, ribs, and bobbles and use raspberry stitch for an allover pattern.

seed stitch

garter stitch

stockinette stitch

cable with bobbles

wide rib

raspberry stitch

◄ patching

Mix knitting with fabric for a contemporary twist to this traditional craft. Keep the patches simple in black and white, ecru, or tones of a single color. Experiment with materials such as suiting and shirting fabrics. Work in blocks and strips, then embellish with stitches by hand or machine to create a truly personal piece.

plying

Create your own random-effect yarns. Take strands of different colored or textured yarns, twist together, and then wind into a ball. Experiment with contrasting shades of black and white for a great marl effect.

unraveling

Seek out alternative sources of yarns and other materials: recycle old sweaters from the back of your closet or discarded knitwear from thrift stores. Launder and reuse them to create new projects. Unravel any knitted fabrics to knit the yarn up again or cut out any interesting details, such as cables or button bands.

redoing

Reassemble knitted pieces into something individual, such as the Customized Cushions (see page 70), mixing different patterns, colors, and stitch textures. Or you may wish to recycle the sleeves of a favorite sweater and add just a newly knitted back and front. Create something unique yet inexpensive!

embroidering

Simple embroidery stitches can be extremely effective for further embellishing knitting.
Embroidery can be used to contrast against the knitted fabric or to complement the
yarn for a subtler result. Use basic running stitches in random lengths to create
a simple pattern on otherwise plain throws and cushions. Give your designs a further
dimension by embroidering with chain stitch or edging a piece of recycled knitting with
basic blanket stitch, at once functional and attractive.

modern
brights

rose chintz cushion

Tradition with a twist! Roses are a perennially popular decorative motif for interiors. This oversize rose chintz cushion creates a little drama for a chair or couch. Worked in really bulky yarn, this shaped cushion takes no time at all to make. The leaves are worked in a melange of greens, and the petal colors can be embroidered after knitting. Backed in a contrasting fabric, this cushion couldn't be easier to create.

see full pattern chart on page 120

making the rose chintz cushion

materials

Rowan *Big Wool*—3½-ounce (100-gram) balls:
  Color A: 2 balls in light pink
  Color B: 1 ball in dark pink
  Color C: 1 ball in black
Rowan *Biggy Print*—3½-ounce (100-gram)
  balls:
  Color D: 1 ball in green melange
1 pair of size 13 (9mm) knitting needles
Blunt-ended sewing needle
Approximately 160 pink sequins
Approximately 150 black sequins
Large sewing needle
Sewing thread
½ yard 36-inch-wide fabric (such as corduroy)
Dressmaker's chalk
Circular pillow form, 16¼ inches in diameter
Velcro for fastening

size

One size (approximately 17¾ inches in diameter)

gauge

10 stitches and 14 rows = 4 inches/10cm in stockinette stitch using size 13 needles. Always work a gauge swatch and change needles accordingly if necessary.

tips

If working the rose as you knit, use the intarsia method; do not strand the yarn across the back of the work as this will distort the image. Use separate lengths of contrasting yarn for the colored areas and twist the yarns together on the wrong side when changing colors to avoid any holes.

knitting the rose

Work the rose in stockinette stitch—one row knit, one row purl alternately—from the chart given on page 120.

Read the chart from right to left on right side (knit) rows and from left to right on wrong side (purl) rows.

Each square on the chart represents a stitch and each row of squares represents a row of knitting.

Cast on and bind off stitches as indicated on the chart to shape the rose. Use a separate ball of yarn for each new color change, twisting the strands of yarn at the back of the work to avoid any holes. (You may wish to wind small balls for separate areas to avoid tangling balls.) You may find it simpler to knit with colors A and D only, then embroider the petals in colors B and C afterward with duplicate stitch. This is a simple method of applying color to a finished piece of knitting. Using duplicate stitch is often quicker, easier, and neater than knitting the colors in, as it leaves you free to concentrate on the knitting at hand.

embroidering the petals

Once you have knitted the basic rose shape, if required, embroider the petal colors B and C with duplicate stitch. The embroidered stitch is worked on top of the knitted stitch in a contrasting color. Using a blunt-ended needle and the required color in a yarn of similar weight, darn in the yarn invisibly at the back. *Then bring the needle up through the center of the stitch from the back of the work, insert the needle from the right to the left, behind the stitch immediately above. Insert the needle through the center of the original stitch and out through the center of the stitch to the left, repeat from *.

sewing on the fabric backing

Weave in all the yarn ends and press flat with a steam iron. Sew on the sequins as shown in the photograph, following the dark pink and black petal shading. Place the rose on the backing fabric, right sides together. With dressmaker's chalk, draw around the shape of the rose. Allowing for a ½-inch seam all the way around, cut the shape out of the fabric. With right sides together, sew the knitted rose and the backing fabric together, leaving an opening at the lower edge large enough to insert the pillow form. Turn the cover right side out and insert the pillow form. Sew Velcro along the opening for easy removal when cleaning.

retro poodle bottle cover

Simply kitsch! This retro look—once the domain of the church rummage sale—is now de rigueur. Adorn your Sixties rosewood dining-room sideboard with the ultimate hostess accessory: a bottle cover for those predinner shots. Knitted in two parts, this cute poodle is made in medium-weight cotton yarn using simple seed stitch. The pompoms really make this design, while the beads for the eyes and embroidery for the nose both add character. And the velvet and diamanté collar? Well, that just finishes it all off. Simply slip the cover over a standard spirit or wine bottle.

making the retro poodle bottle cover

materials

Rowan *Handknit DK Cotton*—1¾-ounce
  (50-gram) balls:
  Color A: 2 balls in pink
  Color B: scraps of yarn in black
1 pair of size 6 (4mm) knitting needles
Large sewing needle
2 small black beads
8 inches black velvet ribbon

size

One size (to fit a standard wine
  or spirit bottle)

gauge

18 stitches and 32 rows = 4 inches/10cm
in seed stitch using size 6 needles. Always
work a gauge swatch and change needles
accordingly if necessary.

knitting the body

With size 6 needles and color A, cast on
17 stitches very loosely.
Row 1: knit to end. **Row 2:** purl to end.
Row 3: * knit 1, increase into next stitch,
repeat from * to last stitch, knit 1.
25 stitches. **Row 4:** purl to end.
Row 5: * knit 2, increase into next
stitch, repeat from * to last stitch, knit 1.
33 stitches.
Row 6: purl to end. **Row 7:** * knit 3,
increase into next stitch, repeat from
* to last stitch, knit 1. *41 stitches.*
Row 8: purl to end.
Change to seed stitch (in other words,
every row, * knit 1, purl 1, repeat from
* to last stitch, knit 1) and continue,
without shaping, until knitting measures
8½ inches or to neck of chosen bottle.
Bind off in seed stitch. Join side seam
using mattress stitch.

knitting the head

With size 6 needles and color A, cast on 33 stitches. Work 10 rows in seed stitch as on body.

Next row: knit 1, purl 1, knit 1, * purl 3 together, knit 1, purl 1, knit 1, repeat from * to end. *23 stitches.*

Continue in seed stitch until knitting measures 4 inches.

Next row: knit 1, purl 1, knit 1, * purl 3 together, knit 1, purl 1, knit 1, repeat from * to last 2 stitches, purl 1, knit 1. *17 stitches.* Work 3 rows in seed stitch.

Next row: knit 1, * purl 3 together, knit 1, repeat from * to end. *9 stitches.* Break off yarn, thread through the remaining stitches and fasten securely. Join side seam using mattress stitch.

knitting the nose

With size 6 needles and color A, cast on 5 stitches. Continue in seed stitch as on body until knitting measures 2½ inches. Bind off in seed stitch.

Sew cast-on edge to bind-off edge. Join one side and stuff with matching yarn. Join other side. Embroider over one end in color B for nose. Sew to head as shown.

knitting the ears

With size 6 needles and color A, cast on 9 stitches. Continue in seed stitch as on body until knitting measures 3½ inches. Bind off in seed stitch.

Slightly gather cast-on and bind-off edges to curve and sew to head as shown.

making the pompoms

You need three different size pompoms— one large for the head, three medium for the ears and tail, and six small, including four for the paws and two for the face.

To make a large pompom: wind the yarn around four fingers 75 times.

To make a medium pompom: wind the yarn around three fingers 60 times.

To make a small pompom: wind the yarn around three fingers 50 times.

Once the yarn has been wound around the requisite number of fingers the required amount of times, remove the yarn from your fingers and tie the bundle tightly in the middle.

Cut through the loops on each side.

Trim to a smooth round shape.

Attach to the body and head as shown.

finishing the poodle

Sew on beads for eyes as shown.

Join ribbon into circle for collar.

recycled plastic carryall

What do you do with mountains of spare plastic shopping bags? Recycle them, of course. Simply collect the bags, cut them into strips, and knit. This knitted carryall is such an easy project once you are used to working with the different textures of plastic. The simple handle is made from leather thonging—looped through the plastic and knotted— to give some precious contrast to the disposable plastic. Use the bag for storage just about anywhere in the home or garden, even in the kitchen as a container for collecting other plastic bags. Experiment with different colors, regular or random stripes, or use just a single color for a completely even, chic look.

making the recycled plastic carryall

materials

Assorted plastic shopping bags, cut into
½-inch-wide strips (see below)

1 pair of size 10½ (6.5 or 7mm) knitting
needles

Multipurpose polypropylene string
(available from hardware stores)

Large sewing needle

3½ yards leather thonging, cut into two
equal lengths of 1¾ yards

size

One size (15 inches high by 12½ inches wide by 7 inches deep)

gauge

14 stitches and 20 rows = 4 inches/10cm in garter stitch using size 10½ needles.
Always work a gauge swatch and change needles accordingly if necessary.

cutting the bags into strips

Cut off the top section of each plastic
bag to remove the handles.

Starting at the open top edge and
cutting through one side at a time, cut
a narrow strip in a spiral all the way
down the bag—a little like peeling an
orange—to make one continuous length.
If the strips are too wide, simply cut
them in half again.

If the strips are too narrow, simply knit
with two strips together.

Knot different color lengths together
as desired.

Wind the strips into balls.

knitting the back

With size 10½ needles, cast on
44 stitches.

Continue in garter stitch (in other
words, knit every row) until knitting
measures 15 inches, ending with a wrong
side row. Bind off.

knitting the front

Work as given for back.

knitting the gusset

With size 10½ needles, cast on
20 stitches.

Continue in garter stitch as on back
until knitting measures 42 inches, ending
with a wrong side row. Bind off.

making up the bag

Starting at one end of gussett,
pin or baste the gusset to the back
around three edges, easing and
straightening to ensure the corners
are square.

Repeat with the front to form the other
side of the bag.

Using polypropylene string and a large
sewing needle, stitch all the way around
the pinned or basted edges with tiny
running stitches. (Do not use backstitch
as this will distort the knitted plastic.)

making the handles

Across the back, mark the position of
the handles with a colored thread—
approximately 4 inches in from each
side of the bag and 1¼ inches from the
top edge.

Thread the leather thonging from the
inside through to the outside of the
knitted bag at one marked point and then
back through at the other marked point.
Thread the thonging through twice more
and knot on the inside of the bag.
Repeat for the front.

woven woolen rug

This knitted rug is the simplest of projects to make for the home, and an economical way of recycling remnants of yarn in the age-old tradition. It's great if you are new to knitting, too, as it really is so quick and easy to make, and a little more functional than most first knitting projects! This is a new take on double knitting, where the different knitted strips are simply woven together to make a stylish textile for the floor. Alternatively, make this rug in tones of one hue to enhance the textures and coordinate with a particular color scheme in your house.

making the woven woolen rug

materials

Assorted yarns from your stash—you
will need approximately 1¾ ounces
(50 grams) of yarn for one strip measuring
32 inches long and 3¾ inches wide)
1 pair of size 10½ (6.5 or 7mm) knitting
  needles, or size for your chosen yarns
Sewing needle
Sewing thread

size

The size of this rug is determined by the length of the knitted strips, which can be
varied as required. The rug shown here measures 32 inches long by 24 inches wide.

gauge

12 stitches and 16 rows = 4 inches/10cm in stockinette stitch using 10½ needles.
Always work a gauge swatch and change needles accordingly if necessary.

making a knitted tube

Cast on an even number of stitches.
(The rug shown here is made of double knitting strips of 20 stitches.)

Row 1: * knit 1, bring yarn to front of work between needles, slip 1 purlwise, take yarn to back of work between needles, repeat from * to end.

The last stitch of every row is a slipped purl stitch.

Repeat this row until knitting measures 32 inches or required length.

Bind off by working 2 stitches together (in other words, knit 2 together, knit 2 together, then slip the first stitch over the second) to end of row.

Thread the yarn end through the last loop and pull to fasten off.

weaving the knitted strips

Once you have made the required number of long and short strips, simply lay them out in a grid with the longer ones running lengthwise and the short ones running widthwise.

Weave all the strips together, working them over and under each other alternately.

Where the lengthwise and widthwise strips cross, secure each strip in place with small stitches using the sewing thread.

patchwork throw

This fun-to-knit, reversible throw is made from three knitted strips, each one consisting of four different blocks alternately worked in stockinette, reverse stockinette, and seed stitch. Yarns are doubled or tripled for bulky effect and quick results. Contrasting borders are worked in double knitting. Use the yarns specified in the pattern, or for your own individual look, work with a mix of leftovers from your stash or the sale bin at your local yarn shop.

blues
greys
purples
cream

see full pattern chart on page 121

making the patchwork throw

materials

Use a mixture of yarns for textural effect. Use one strand of yarn on its own, or two or three strands together, to achieve the correct weight and gauge (see page 25). The following yarns were used to make the throw shown here:

Sirdar *Supa Nova Chunky*—3½-ounce (100-gram) balls
   Color A: 3 balls in mid pink (two strands)
Rowan *Como*—1¾-ounce (50-gram) balls
   Color B: 7 balls in white (three strands)
Rowan *Polar*—1¾-ounce (50-gram) balls
   Color C: 4 balls in purple (two strands)
Jaeger *Cadiz Cotton*—1¾-ounce (50-gram) balls
   Color D: 3 balls in bright pink (three strands)

Rowan *Biggy Print*—3½-ounce (100-gram) balls
   Color E: 5 balls in multi pink (one strand)
Rowan *Como*—1¾-ounce (50-gram) balls
   Color F: 7 balls in light pink (three strands)
Rowan *Cork*—1¾-ounce (50-gram) balls
   Color G: 5 balls in black (two strands)
1 pair of size 11 (8mm) knitting needles and 1 pair of size 13 (9mm) knitting needles
Large sewing needle

size

One size (66 inches long by 52 inches wide)

gauge

8 stitches and 10 rows = 4 inches/10cm in stockinette stitch using size 13 needles. Always work a gauge swatch and change needles accordingly if necessary.

tips

Do not worry about color changes showing; it is a deliberate feature to add contrast.

preparing the yarns

Ply two or three strands of your selected yarns together to make one bulky yarn. If the yarn is already bulky, you may only need to use a single strand.

knitting the first strip of blocks

With size 13 needles and color A, cast on 34 stitches. Work the throw from the chart given on page 121. Read the chart from right to left on right side rows and from left to right on wrong side rows. Each square on the chart represents a stitch and each row on the chart represents a row of knitting.

Row 1: work across 1st row of chart for first strip in color A, working in seed stitch as indicated.

Row 2: work across 2nd row of chart for first strip in color A, working in seed stitch as indicated.

Continue as established, working in stockinette stitch, reverse stockinette stitch, or seed stitch and changing yarn where indicated until first strip is complete. Bind off.

knitting the second and third strips

Work as for first strip, following chart for second or third strip as appropriate.

knitting the borders

With size 11 needles and color E, cast on 16 stitches.

Row 1: * knit 1, bring yarn to front of work between needles, slip 1 purlwise, take yarn to back of work between needles, repeat from * to end.
Repeat this row until knitting measures 60 inches or same length as knitted strips. Bind off by working 2 stitches together (in other words, knit 2 together, knit 2

together, slip first stitch over second) to end of row. Thread the yarn end through the last loop and pull to fasten off. Make another border in the same way to the same length using color A. Make two further border strips using yarn B and yarn F but to the shorter length of 52 inches or the same width as the three strips plus the first two borders.

finishing the throw

Weave in all the yarn ends and block all strips with a steam iron, taking care not to flatten the stitch textures. Sew the strips of blocks together lengthwise using a single strand of yarn in a contrasting color. Sew the borders to the edges of the throw, attaching the longer pieces first. Butt up the shorter border pieces to the top and bottom of the throw and sew in place.

black
and
whites

wall hangings

Knitting doesn't only have to be worn. Simple knitted pieces can be stretched over a canvas or frame and hung on the wall. Here, the op-art paintings of the Sixties have been reinvented with simple knitted patterns for interior decoration. The flower, stripe, and block designs are all in graphic black and white, which could be further embellished with chain-stitch embroidery. There are three different sizes given here, but it is such a simple principle that you could make hangings to any size or shape. Here they have been worked in cotton for stitch clarity, but they could be made in any yarn, and embroidered, appliquéd, or even felted for extra dimension. Either work the design into the piece or knit a plain background and duplicate-stitch the pattern on afterward.

see full pattern chart on page 122

making the wall hangings

materials
Rowan *DK Cotton*—1¾-ounce
  (50-gram) balls
flower
  Color A: 6 balls in ecru
  Color B: 2 balls in black
  Color C: scraps in orange
stripes
  Color A: 2 balls in ecru
  Color B: 1 ball in black
blocks
  Color A: 2 balls in ecru
  Color B: 1 ball in black
Ready-made canvas, frame, or plywood
  cut to size
1 pair of size 5 (3.75mm) knitting needles
Large sewing needle

size
flower 18 inches x 18 inches
stripes 10 inches x 10 inches
blocks 6 inches x 6 inches

gauge
20 stitches and 28 rows = 4 inches/10cm in stockinette stitch using size 5 needles.
Always work a gauge swatch and change needles accordingly if necessary.

tips
Work the design using the Intarsia method, do not strand the yarn across the back of the work as this will distort the image. Use separate lengths of contrasting yarn for the colored areas and twist the yarns together on the wrong side when changing colors to avoid any holes.

knitting the flower design
With size 5 needles and color A, cast on 90 stitches. Work 22 rows in stockinette stitch—one row knit, one row purl alternately.
Cast on 15 stitches at the beginning of the next 2 rows and at the same time work the flower from the chart given on page 122 starting on the 16th stitch of each row.
Read the chart from right to left on right side (knit) rows and from left to right on wrong side (purl) rows. Each square on the chart represents a stitch and each row of squares represents a row of knitting.
You may find it simpler to knit with color A only, then embroider the flower in color B afterwards with duplicate stitch. Bind off 15 stitches at the beginning of the next 2 rows. *90 stitches.*

Change to color A and work 22 rows in stockinette stitch. Bind off.

embroidering with chain stitch
Lay a length of yarn over the knitted design, allowing it to curl and twist, then baste or tape it in position and follow the line in chain stitch. Alternatively, crochet a long chain, lay over the design, and stitch in position.

knitting the stripe design
With size 5 needles and color A, cast on 50 stitches. Work 22 rows in stockinette stitch as on flower design.
Cast on 15 stitches at the beginning of the next 2 rows and at the same time work the stripes from the chart given on page 123 starting on the 16th stitch of each row. Bind off 15 stitches at the beginning of the next 2 rows. *50 stitches.*

Change to color A and work 22 rows in stockinette stitch. Bind off.

knitting the block design
With size 5 needles and color A, cast on 30 stitches. Work 22 rows in stockinette stitch as on flower design.
Cast on 15 stitches at the beginning of the next 2 rows and at the same time work the blocks from the chart given on page 123 starting on the 16th stitch of each row. Bind off 15 stitches at the beginning of the next 2 rows. *30 stitches.*
Change to color A and work 22 rows in stockinette stitch. Bind off.

finishing the wall hangings
Weave in all the yarn ends and press flat with a steam iron. Lay the knitted design over the ready-made canvas, stretch into position, and staple securely at the back.

barcode dog coat

Good and loyal pals deserve a little knitted attention, too! So what better than this barcode dog coat for your more-than-fair-weather friend. Knitted in one piece, the coat can be embroidered with your telephone number; after all you would want him to be safely returned should he choose to stray. Patterned in random stripes in graphic black and white, the coat is worked in stockinette stitch with a detailed rib rollneck for a little rakish style. It is easy to pull over a dog's head without ties or buttons, nips or yelps!

making the barcode dog coat

materials
Rowan *Wool Cotton*—1¾-ounce
  (50-gram) balls
  Color A: 2 balls in black
  Color B: 1 ball in ecru
1 pair of size 5 (3.75mm) knitting needles
1 pair of size 6 (4mm) knitting needles
2 stitch holders or safety pins
Large sewing needle

size
One size (approximately 15-inch chest and 13½ inches long)

gauge
22 stitches and 32 rows = 4 inches/10cm in stockinette stitch using size 6 needles.
Always work a gauge swatch and change needles accordingly if necessary.

tips
The dog coat is worked in one piece in stockinette stitch, with random stripes of 1, 2, or 3 rows in colors A and B alternately. Break off and rejoin yarns as necessary. When binding off around neck edge, use larger size knitting needles to keep the rib loose and flexible.

knitting the body
Using size 5 needles and color A, cast on 49 stitches. Work 3 rows in single rib (in other words, * knit 1, purl 1, repeat from * to last stitch, knit 1). Change to size 6 needles and stockinette stitch, work in random stripes of 1, 2, or 3 rows but place plain band as follows:

Row 1: with color A, knit to end.
Row 2: with color A, purl 11, change to color B, purl to end.
Continue pattern as set but at the same time increase 1 stitch at each end of next and every alternate row to 75 stitches. Increase 1 stitch at each end of every 3rd row to 83 stitches. Mark last row with colored thread. Work even until knitting measures 7¼ inches, ending with a wrong side row.
Divide leg openings: knit 14, turn.
Next row: bind off 2 stitches, purl to end.

Work 23 rows on these 12 stitches.
Break off yarn and place stitches on stitch holder. With right side facing, rejoin yarn.
Next row: knit 55, turn.
Work 24 rows on these 55 stitches.
Break off yarn and place stitches on stitch holder. With right side facing, rejoin yarn.
Next row: bind off 2 stitches, knit to end.
Work 24 rows on these 12 stitches.
Next row: purl 12, cast on 2 stitches, purl 55 from stitch holder, cast on 2 stitches, purl 12 from stitch holder. *83 stitches.*
Shape neck: knit 10, knit 2 tog, knit 2, knit 2 tog through back loop, knit 51, knit 2 tog, knit 2, knit 2 tog through back loop, knit to end. *79 stitches.*
Next row: purl to end. **Next row:** knit 9, knit 2 tog, knit 2, knit 2 tog through back loop, knit 49, knit 2 tog, knit 2, knit 2 tog through back loop, knit to end. *75 stitches.*
Next row: purl to end.

Continue decreasing as set until 63 stitches remain.
Next row: purl 30, purl 2 tog, purl to end. *62 stitches.*
Knit collar: using color B, work 4 inches in single rib as on body.
Bind off loosely in rib.

finishing the dog coat
Weave in all yarn ends and press flat with a steam iron. Referring to chart, embroider telephone number on plain band in duplicate stitch. Join seam from collar to colored thread. With size 5 needles and color B, pick up and knit 67 stitches around inner bottom edge. Work 3 rows in single rib as on body. Bind off loosely. With size 5 needles and color B, pick up and knit 21 stitches along side of left leg. Work 5 rows in single rib. Bind off loosely. Repeat along both sides of leg openings. Join edges of rib.

patched throw

Using scraps of fabric to create patchwork is a traditional way to recycle. Here, however, patchwork has the addition of pieces of knitting, which have been recycled in their turn by plying ends together to create new yarns (see page 25). The simple theme of black and white adds a modern dimension to patchwork, and will look dynamic in most interiors. The instructions given here are for inspiration. Select fabrics of your choice in patches of suitable shapes and size, then tailor your knitted pieces to complement and add texture and interest.

making the patched throw

materials

fabrics: Keep it simple by using a limited number of fabrics—no more than 5 or 6 different types—as either the patchwork pieces or the appliqué. The throw shown here uses a striped fabric, a firm striped cotton used for mattresses, a white wool (also used for the backing), a houndstooth check, and a woven.

yarns: Likewise, keep the knitting simple by limiting the yarns to 2 or 3 and using basic stitches—stockinette stitch, garter stitch, seed stitch, ribbing, or slip stitches. Also, use the yarns as decoration in the form of running stitches, knots, and tufts. The throw shown here uses ecru wool-cotton, tweed wool, and black chenille yarns.

trims: The throw shown here uses plaid ribbon, gingham ribbon, and scraps of the various fabrics for the appliqué.
1 pair of size 13 (9mm) knitting needles
Large sewing needle
Sewing thread
Iron-on cotton interfacing

size

The size of the throw is determined by the size and shape of the patchwork pieces, which can be varied as required. The throw shown here measures 47 inches by 41 inches.

gauge

12 stitches and 20 rows = 4 inches/10cm in stockinette stitch using size 13 needles. Always work a gauge swatch and change needles accordingly if necessary.

planning the throw

Using graph paper, work out the desired dimensions of the throw, including the distribution of the fabric and knitted pieces so you can see how to separate plains, stripes, and knits. Sample the decorative effects on your fabrics.

cutting the fabric pieces

Cut all fabric pieces with a 1-inch seam allowance all the way around. Back each piece of fabric with iron-on cotton interfacing (this helps to hold the shape).

decorating the fabric pieces

Decorate each fabric piece separately using a combination of effects:
a) Use the selvage of the fabrics, as they often give a "fancy" effect.
b) Fringe woven fabrics to make wide, narrow strips or squares and oblongs.

These can then be topstitched on.
c) Draw threads out of the fabrics, either main pieces or smaller decorative ones.
d) Knit small patches or strips and zigzag stitch on by hand or using a machine.
e) Tie bows of ribbons, cord, twine, or frayed fabrics through the main pieces.
f) Use knitting yarns to sew uneven running stitches through the patchwork pieces to link them together.

making the knitted pieces

Knit the appropriate size pieces (test your gauge first) and remember to include some seam allowance. As with the fabric pieces, back each knitted piece with iron-on cotton interfacing.

putting the throw together

Referring to your plan for positioning, hand- or machine-stitch the pieces together.

backing the throw

Cut a piece of woolen fabric, such as an old blanket, to the size of the patchwork plus seam allowance. Place the patchwork right side up on top of the backing fabric and machine-stitch around the edge.

quilting the throw

Apply any running stitches through the patchwork and backing fabric. Topstitch all patchwork pieces by machine or hand along the seams. Machine-stitch on any extra decorative appliqués and add any wool embroidery.

finishing the throw

Add a ribbon edge or strips of contrasting fabric by sandwiching the throw in between the ribbon and butting up the ribbon ends at the corners of the throw.

laddered sweater

A favorite sweater is often regarded as an "old friend," but there comes a time when it is beyond repair and, quite frankly, has seen far better days. But what makes you hold onto it? Its comfort, warmth, and smell of familiarity makes you feel secure. It may have been a gift from a friend or family member, which creates a certain sentimental attachment. Well, this laddered sweater strikes a similar chord. Knitted in soft, comfortable wool, and with a well-worn, loved feel, it looks great and retains a certain urban appeal. The exaggerated ladders incorporated into the body of the sweater make amazing patterns— you could add more to make a "cobweb" sweater or devise your own. Ladders are not a new technique in knitting, however. They were a feature of knitting even in the Victorian era, used for great decorative and intricate effect. Here I have just taken the idea a little bit further to give this sweater a deconstructed look.

making the laddered sweater

materials
Rowan *Chunky Merino*—1¾-ounce (50-gram) balls
 Color A: 19 balls in ecru
 Color B: 1 ball in black
1 pair of size 10½ (6.5mm) knitting needles
Stitch holder or safety pin
Large sewing needle

size
small/medium   chest: 45 inches   length: 27 inches
medium/large   chest: 48 inches   length: 28½ inches

gauge
13½ stitches and 19 rows = 4 inches/10cm in stockinette
stitch using size 10½ needles. Always work a gauge swatch
and change needles accordingly if necessary.

knitting the back
Using size 10½ needles and color A, cast
on 66 (76) stitches. Work 2 rows in single
rib (in other words, knit 1, purl 1 to end).
Change to stockinette stitch and
increase 1 stitch at each end of 19th row
and every following 20th row to 74 (84)
stitches. Work even until knitting
measures 16¾ (17¾) inches ending with
a wrong side row.
Shape armhole: bind off 4 (5) stitches
at beginning of next 2 rows.
Decrease 1 stitch at each end of next and
every alternate row until 58 (66) stitches
remain. Continue without shaping until
piece measures 25 (27) inches ending
with wrong side row.
Shape shoulders and neck: knit to last
5 (6) stitches, turn.
Next row: slip first stitch, purl to last
5 (6) stitches, turn.

Next row: slip first stitch, knit to last
10 (12) stitches, turn.
Next row: slip first stitch, purl 4 (5)
stitches, turn.
Next row: bind off 15 (18) stitches.
Break off yarn.
With wrong side facing, rejoin yarn.
Bind off 28 (30) stitches loosely purlwise,
purl next 4 (5) stitches, turn. *5 (6) stitches.*
Next row: slip first stitch, knit to end.
Bind off 15 (18) stitches loosely purlwise.

knitting the front
Using size 10½ needles and color A, cast
on 66 (76) stitches.
Work 2 rows in single rib as on back.
Change to stockinette stitch and
increase 1 stitch at each end of 19th row
and every following 20th row to 74 (84)
stitches, but at the same time make the
random irregular ladders as follows:

Row 3 (ladder 1): knit 19, m1 (in other
words, pick up the loop between stitches
and knit into the back).
Row 5 (ladder 2): knit 33, m1.
Row 7 (ladder 3): knit 52, m1.
Row 11: knit 20, m1.
Row 13: knit 35, m1.
Row 17 (ladder 4): knit 9, m1, m1.
Row 19: knit 23, m1.
Row 25 (ladder 5): knit 31, m1.
Row 29: drop first m1 to right of ladder 1.
Row 31 (ladder 6): knit 70, m1.
Row 41: drop m1 to left of ladder 2.
Row 43: drop ladder 2, drop m1 to left of
ladder 1.
Row 45: drop ladder 1, m1 to left of
ladder 6.
Row 51: drop m1 to right of ladder 4.
Row 55: drop ladder 6.
Row 63: m1 before ladder 5.
Row 69: drop ladder 3.

Row 71: drop ladder 4.

Row 83: drop ladder 5.

Continue until armhole shaping is complete as given for back and piece measures 23¼ (25¼) inches ending with wrong side row.

Shape neck: knit 20 (22), leave remaining stitches on stitch holder.

Next row: purl to end.

Decrease 1 stitch at neck edge on next and every alternate row until 15 (18) stitches remain.

Shape shoulder: purl to last 5 (6) stitches, turn.

Next row: slip first stitch, knit to end, turn.

Next row: purl 5 (6) stitches, turn.

Next row: slip first stitch, knit to end. Bind off 15 (18) stitches.

With right side facing, rejoin yarn.

Next row: bind off 18 (22) stitches, knit to end.

Purl 1 row, complete to match first side, reversing all shaping.

knitting the sleeves (make 2)

Using size 10½ needles and color A, cast on 40 (43) stitches.

Work in knit 5, purl 3 rib for 2 inches as follows:

Row 1: Purl 0 (3), [knit 5, purl 3] to end.

Row 2: [knit 3, purl 5] to last 3 stitches, knit 0 (3).

Continuing in rib, increase 1 stitch at each end of next and every following 8th row to 58 (61) stitches.

(Increase using make 1 method rather than knitting twice into one stitch.)

Continue without shaping until piece measures 17 (18) inches ending with wrong side row.

Shape top: bind off 4 (5) stitches at beginning of next 2 rows.

Decrease 1 stitch each end of next and

every alternate row until 14 (13) stitches remain.

Next row: knit 3, purl 2 tog, work across rib as set to last 5 stitches, purl 2 tog, knit 3. Decrease 1 stitch each end of every row until 6 (7) stitches remain. Bind off.

knitting the collar

With size 10½ needles and color A, cast on 64 (74) stitches. Work 3¼ inches in single rib. Change to color B and bind off loosely.

finishing the sweater

Weave in all the yarn ends and block flat with a steam iron. Sew shoulder seams. Set sleeves into armholes between shaping and sew with mattress stitch, easing in the ribs as you sew. Sew sleeve and side seams. Sew collar with fine backstitch so that the seam will show on the outside. Run ladders down.

customized cushions

Unraveling sweaters and other items of knitwear and then using that yarn to create something else was once a common practice. Now we have no shortage of new products to buy or material to make things from. However, this practice of recycling can be incredibly creative and spark great individual ideas. Seek out old pieces of knitwear from rummage sales, thrift shops, or from the back of your closet, then cut up and reorganize the pieces. Cushions, especially, are among the easiest and cheapest items to assemble in this way. Combine stripes, stitches, colors, patterns, and textures, and bring a little seasonal touch and personality to your interior.

making the customized cushions

materials
Discarded knitted items in wool or cotton, incorporating where possible stitch details —especially ribs, cables, and Arans—for texture, or patterns—such as Fair Isle, argyle, or plaids—for color
Pillow forms of various sizes
Large sewing needle
Sewing machine
Pencil
Paper
Pins
Velcro, snaps, or tapes

size
The sizes of the cushions are determined by the size of the pillow forms, which can be varied as required. The cushions shown here measure 20 inches by 20 inches, 15 inches by 15 inches, and 20 inches by 12 inches.

tips
Alternatively knit some squares or rectangles using remnants of yarn in addition to recycled pieces. You may wish to add a specific detail, such as a big cable or a seed-stitch panel. Try the stitch textures given for the Aran Armchair Cover on pages 101–102.

making the cushion front
Draw around the pillow form to make a template for the cushion cover. Using the template as a guide, cut the knitted items into strips, squares, rectangles, or other shapes to fit the shape of your cushion when put all together. There is no need to allow for a seam, as the cushion cover will fit better if slightly stretched over the pillow form.
You may wish to incorporate necklines or full-fashion details in your design for added interest.
Once you have cut the cushion cover pieces, either blanket stitch all around each piece by hand or alternatively overlock on the sewing machine.
Press all the pieces flat with a steam iron. Lay out the pieces in a design of your choice.

Sew together by hand or machine to make the shape of the template.

finishing the cushion
Cut a piece from a knitted item the same size as your pillow form or template. Overlock all around the backing piece. With right sides together, sew the backing fabric to the cushion cover front, leaving an opening large enough to insert the pillow form at the lower edge. Turn the cover right side out and insert the pillow form. Neaten up the cushion opening, attaching Velcro, snaps, or tapes for easy removal when cleaning. Alternatively, cut two pieces of knitted fabric for the cushion backing that make up the shape of the template when overlapped in the center. Overlock all around each backing piece. With right sides together, sew the two

overlapping backing pieces to the cushion cover front. Turn the cover right side out and insert the pillow form. Alternatively, incorporate the button band of a discarded cardigan into the design of your cushion front and back, making sure the buttons and buttonholes match up when making up the cushion. You can further customize each cushion by adding embroidery or other embellishments, such as beads or sequins.

urban
neutrals

beaded napkin rings

Worked in wire adorned with iridescent beads, these quick and easy napkin rings make a unique addition to the urban tabletop. Knit one in a different color for each person in the family or make a matching set for a special party or dinner. Contrast with matte linen or sumptuous shantung silk napkins.

making the beaded napkin rings

materials

Amounts given are for one napkin ring

7¾ yards (23 feet) colored artistic wire,
   24 gauge (.5mm)

Approximately 120 iridescent beads,
   4mm in diameter, in a complementary
   or contrasting color

1 pair of size 9 (5.5mm) knitting needles

size

One size (each napkin ring measures 7 inches by 2 inches)

gauge

10 stitches and 12 rows = 4 inches/10cm in garter stitch using size 9 knitting needles.
Always work a gauge swatch and change needles accordingly if necessary.

tips

It is important to thread the correct number of beads (or a few more than necessary)
onto the wire before starting to knit. Once the wire coil is started, it is difficult to add
more beads unless threaded from the other end of the wire or by breaking off the wire,
adding more beads, then rejoining the wire.

threading the beads

Check that the wire will pass through
the beads.
Make a small loop at one end of the wire
and twist so that the beads will stay on.
Thread the beads onto the wire.

knitting the bands

Cast on 16 stitches, putting one bead on
every stitch as you cast on. As you bring
the wire around to make a stitch, slide up
a bead first.
Knit to the end of the row, sliding up
a bead for each stitch knitted. Again,
as you bring the wire around to make
a stitch, slide up a bead first.
Knit 7 rows in garter stitch in this way.
Bind off, putting a bead on every stitch
as you bind off.
Leave a long end (approximately 5 inches) to
use when joining the knitted band into a ring.

finishing the napkin rings

Bend the knitted band into a ring and
thread the long end of the wire all along
the seam to fasten together.

satin boudoir slippers

Ribbon is a beautiful and readily available material for knitting. There
is a huge variety currently on the market, from satins, velvets, and
organzas to ginghams and brocades. These simple slippers are worked
in two stockinette-stitch pieces in a double-sided satin ribbon that
creates a luxurious yet firm fabric. Lined with an insole covered in silk
dupion and decoratively adorned with ribbon ties, they are both pretty
and practical.

making the satin boudoir slippers

materials

Amounts given are for one pair of slippers
Approximately 95 (100: 110) yards
  ½-inch-wide double-sided satin ribbon
1 pair of size 9 (5.5mm) knitting needles
Large sewing needle
Pair of insoles
Approximately ¼ yard 27-inch-wide
  silk dupion
Fabric glue

size

small	shoe size: 4½–5½	actual length: 8¼ inches
medium	shoe size: 6½–7½	actual length: 9 inches
large	shoe size: 8½–9½	actual length: 9¾ inches

gauge

14 stitches and 19 rows = 4 inches/10cm in stockinette stitch using size 9 needles. Always work a gauge swatch and change needles accordingly if necessary.

knitting the sole and heel

With size 9 needles, cast on 6 (8: 10) stitches. Work 2 rows in stockinette stitch (in other words, knit 1 row, purl 1 row). Increase 1 stitch at each end of next and every alternate row to 12 (14: 16) stitches. Continue in stockinette stitch until knitting measures 8¼ (9: 9¾) inches ending with wrong side row.
Decrease 1 stitch at each end of next and every alternate row until 6 (8: 10) stitches remain.
Next row (right side row): purl to end. (This row makes the ridge where the heel is folded.)
Next row: increase 1 stitch at each end of next and every alternate row to 12 (14: 16) stitches.
Next row: purl to end.
Cast on 8 (8: 8) stitches at the beginning of the next 2 rows. *28 (30: 32) stitches.*

Work 2 additional rows in stockinette stitch.
Next row: decrease 1 stitch at each end of next 4 rows. *20 (22: 24) stitches.* Bind off.

knitting the upper

With size 9 needles, cast on 6 (8: 10) stitches. Work 2 rows in stockinette stitch as on sole.
Increase 1 stitch at each end of next and every alternate row to 12 (14: 16) stitches.
Next row: purl to end.
Next row: knit 3, make 1 by picking up loop between next stitch, knit to last 3 stitches, make 1, knit to end.
Continue increasing in this way on every knit row to 20 (22: 24) stitches. Continue in stockinette stitch until knitting measures 4¾ (5⅛: 5½) inches. Bind off.

finishing the slippers

Weave in all yarn ends and press flat with a steam iron. With wrong sides facing, fold at the heel line and sew each side of the heel to the sole creating the seam on the outside. Pin the upper in position, overlapping the side points, and stitch, securing the overlap with an extra stitch. Attach ribbon to the sides for ties.

making the insoles

Cut insoles to the required shoe size. Trace around the insoles on the silk dupion, leaving a ½-inch allowance, and cut out the fabric shapes. Cover the top of the insoles with the cut fabric and glue in place on underside.
Cut 2 additional insole shapes from the fabric but without the ½-inch allowance. Glue in place on the underside of the insoles covering any raw fabric edges. Allow glue to dry thoroughly before inserting into finished slipper.

painted felt cushion

The top of this cushion is made with an out-of-the-ordinary, homemade yarn: a piece of felt embellished with metallic paint, then cut into one long strip and wound into a ball. The pillow backing is made from the same felt but, in this case, is left in its natural, uncut fabric form. Use this simple technique to create your own personalized yarns of different colors and textures.

making the painted felt cushion

materials

Approximately 2¼ yards wool felt,
  27 inches wide
Fabric paint in complementary or
  contrasting color and paintbrush
1 pair of size 9 (5.5mm) knitting needles
Large sewing needle
Sewing thread
Pillow form, 18 inches square

size

One size (each cushion measures 18 inches by 18 inches)

gauge

6 stitches and 8 rows = 4 inches/10cm in stockinette stitch using size 9 needles.
Always work a gauge swatch and change needles accordingly if necessary.

tips

You may find it easier to cut the felt into a few pieces before painting. If you do this, don't worry about getting a seamless join when adding in a new length of yarn as the knitted surface will be highly textural.

making the cushion back

Cut two pieces of felt 18 inches wide by 15½ inches long.
Overlap these two pieces so that they make a square measuring 18 inches by 18 inches. Pin in position.

painting and cutting the felt

Lay the remainder of the felt out flat. Using a paintbrush, paint horizontal stripes on to the felt approximately 1 inch apart. Allow to dry.
Working from right to left, cut the felt into a strip along the first painted stripe almost to the left edge, but leaving approximately ¾ inch. Change direction and cut along the second painted stripe, again leaving approximately ¾ inch at the right edge. Cut the rest of the felt in this way to make one continuous length of fabric.

knitting the cushion front

With size 9 knitting needles, cast on 24 stitches.
Continue in stockinette stitch—one row knit, one row purl alternately—until knitting measures 18 inches.
Bind off.

finishing the cushion

Pin the cushion backs to the reverse side of the knitted cushion front. You may prefer the reverse stockinette stitch side to the stockinette stitch side, it's your choice.
Stitch seams all the way around on the right side, either by hand or by machine, to leave a pronounced external seam.
Insert the pillow form through the back flap opening.

molded wire bowls

Wire has often been used for knitting, most spectacularly in the arena of costume design for the theater. Surprisingly, wire is very easy to knit with and is available in the most stunning colors. Worked on two needles and in simple stockinette stitch, knitted fabric takes on a wholly different character in wire. The very best part of this project is shaping the bowl once it is knitted—mold it, twist it, bend it, fold it, distort it, personalize it. Use the bowl to hold bonbons or jewelry, or make several in different sizes, shapes, and colors and cluster them together. Experiment.

making the
molded wire bowls

materials

Amounts given are for one bowl

1 (3) x 50-gram (30 yards) reels of colored
   artistic wire, 24 gauge (.5mm)

1 pair of size 9 (5.5mm) knitting needles

size

small   height: 4¾ inches
            circumference: 17 inches

large   height: 4¾ inches
            circumference: 21 inches

gauge

14 stitches and 17 rows = 4 inches/10cm
in stockinette stitch using size 9 needles.
Always work a gauge swatch and change
needles accordingly if necessary.

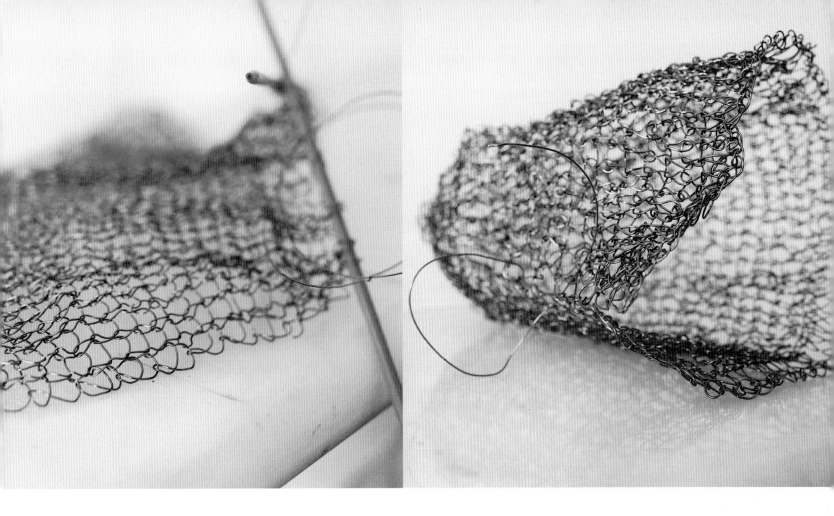

knitting the bowl

Cast on 61 (75) stitches.

Work 4 rows in stockinette stitch—one row knit, one row purl alternately.

Next row: * knit 8, knit 2 together, repeat from * to last 1 (5) stitches, knit 1 (5). *55 (68) stitches.*

Work 3 rows in stockinette stitch.

Next row: * knit 7, knit 2 together, repeat from * to last 1 (5) stitches, knit 1 (5). *49 (61) stitches.*

Work 3 rows in stockinette stitch.

Next row: * knit 6, knit 2 together, repeat from * to last 1 (5) stitches, knit 1 (5). *43 (54) stitches.*

Work 3 rows in stockinette stitch.

Next row: * knit 5, knit 2 together, repeat from * to last 1 (5) stitches, knit 1 (5). *37 (47) stitches.*

Next row: purl to end.

Next row: * knit 4, knit 2 together, repeat from * to last 1 (5) stitches, knit 1 (5). *31 (40) stitches.*

Next row: knit to end. (This row makes the ridge that forms the base.)

Next row: * knit 3, knit 2 together, repeat from * to last 1 (0) stitch, knit 1 (0). *25 (32) stitches.*

Next row: purl to end.

Next row: * knit 2, knit 2 together, repeat from * to last 1 (0) stitch, knit 1 (0). *19 (24) stitches.*

Next row: purl to end.

Next row: * knit 1, knit 2 together, repeat from * to last 1 (0) stitch, knit 1 (0). *13 (16) stitches.*

Next row: purl to end.

Next row: * purl 2 together, repeat from * to last 1 (0) stitch, purl 1 (0). *7 (8) stitches.*

Do not bind off but leave a long end (approximately 6 inches) to use when joining the knitting into a bowl.

finishing the bowl

Bend the knitted bowl so the edges are together and thread the long end of the wire through the remaining stitches on the needle.

Pull the stitches up tight.

Thread the wire all along the edges to fasten together.

Mold the bowl by gently pulling into shape.

flower-trimmed evening bag

Beautifully feminine and totally frivolous! This little bag is knitted
on large needles with net fabric cut into strips. It is made from a
long rectangular shape worked in simple garter stitch and then sewn
together. The corners are folded in and stitched to make a gusset.
It is lined in a sumptuous tonal satin, trimmed with sueded ribbon
handles, and decorated with wired ribbon and a flower corsage made
of net. It is easy to make but enormously effective. Alternatively, make
it in black for added glamour or in vivid vibrant colors just for fun.
The perfect girlish accessory.

making the flower-trimmed evening bag

materials

Approximately 7¾ yards net fabric,
 27 inches wide, cut into 1-inch-wide
 strips (see below)
1 pair of size 13 (9mm) knitting needles
Scraps of net and organza for flower
Approximately 200 iridescent sequins
 for flower
1¾ yards 1½-inch-wide wired ribbon
 for trim
1 yard 1-inch-wide sueded ribbon
 for handles
½ yard 27-inch-wide satin fabric for lining
Sewing needle
Sewing thread

size

One size (bag measures approximately 12½ inches wide by 9¾ inches deep)

gauge

14 stitches and 21 rows = 4 inches/10cm in garter stitch using size 13 needles.
Always work a gauge swatch and change needles accordingly if necessary.

tips

Net can be a little slippery and springy, and has a tendency to move around when being cut. Don't worry if some strips end up wider or thinner than others.

cutting the net

Lay the net out flat. Working from right to left, cut the net into a strip about 1 inch wide almost to the left edge, leaving approximately ¾ inch uncut. Change direction and cut along the net making a 1-inch-wide strip, again leaving approximately ¾ inch at the right edge. Cut the rest of the net in this way to make one continuous length of fabric.

knitting the bag

With size 13 knitting needles, cast on 41 stitches. Continue in garter stitch—knit every row—until knitting measures 24 inches. Bind off. Use the knitted outer as a template to cut the satin lining to the same size, plus an extra ½-inch seam allowance.

finishing the bag

Fold the knitting in half widthwise.

Join side seams by hand or machine. To form the bag's base and gusset, take the tips of the sewn corners and fold inwards to form a box shape (like wrapping the edges of a parcel). Catch the fold corners to the base with a few stitches. Turn right side out.

attaching the handles

Stitch the ribbon handles to the inside of the bag approximately 4 inches apart and 4 inches in from the side edge.

lining the bag

With right sides together, fold the cut satin in half widthwise. As with the knitted outer, sew side seams by hand or machine then create the base and gusset in the same way. Catch the folded corners to the base of the lining with a few stitches. Place the lining inside the

knitted outer, with the right side visible. Fold the top ½ inch of the lining inside the bag to neaten. Hand stitch lining to top edge of bag to secure.

making the flower

Cut rounded bow shapes from the scraps of net and organza for the petals. Add sequins to the edges of each cut petal. Layer the sequin-trimmed petals one on top of the other, alternating the net and organza, and mold into shape. Stitch petals together at the center.

attaching the trim

Wrap the wired ribbon around the bag approximately 2 inches down from the top and tie in a simple bow. Stitch in position. Sew the corsage flower in position on the bag near the ribbon bow to suggest leaves.

organic naturals

aran armchair cover

A wooly sweater for your favorite armchair! Great to cuddle into on chilly afternoons, this loose chair cover is really much easier to knit than first impressions suggest. It is worked in bulky natural tweed wool to parody the classic fisherman's sweater, incorporating traditional patterns that are oversized for increased impact. To keep it manageable, each panel is worked separately with very simple shaping. This cover fits a classic tub chair from Ikea, which is widely available, but with a little alteration can be adapted to cover a chair of a slightly different shape.

making the aran armchair cover

materials

22 3½-ounce (100-gram) hanks Rowan *Rowanspun Chunky* in ecru

1 pair of size 10½ (6.5 or 7mm) knitting needles

Cable needle

Approximately 2¼ yards cotton tape, cut into 10-inch lengths

Large sewing needle

Cotton sewing thread

Tullsta tub chair from Ikea

size

One size (approximately 31½ inches wide, 28½ inches deep, 30¾ inches high, and 17 inches cushion depth)

gauge

13½ stitches and 19 rows = 4 inches/10cm in stockinette stitch using size 10½ needles. Always work a gauge swatch and change needles accordingly if necessary.

tips

When knitting the aran pattern, it is possible to knit the bobbles separately, leave them on a long thread and sew in place when finishing.

When shaping, mark the first increase or decrease with a colored thread so you can see on which side they have been made.

You will need the following stitches to knit the Aran Armchair Cover:

reverse stockinette stitch
Row 1 (right side): purl.
Row 2: knit.
Repeat the last 2 rows.

seed stitch
On an odd number of stitches:
Every row: * knit 1, purl 1, repeat from * to last stitch, knit 1.
On an even number of stitches:
Row 1: * knit 1, purl 1, repeat from * to end.
Row 2: * purl 1, knit 1, repeat from * to end.
Repeat the last 2 rows.

raspberry stitch
The following stitch forms part of the raspberry stitch pattern:
m2 (make 2 stitches): knit 1, purl 1, knit 1 all into next stitch.

Worked over 4 stitches:
Row 1 (right side): purl.
Row 2: knit 1, * m2, purl 3 together [bobble], repeat from * to last stitch, knit 1.
Row 3: purl.
Row 4: knit 1, * purl 3 together, m2, repeat from * to last stitch, knit 1.
Repeat the last 4 rows.

twisted stitch
The following stitch forms part of the twisted stitch pattern:
tw2 (twist 2 stitches): knit second stitch but leave on left-hand needle, then knit first stitch, slip both stitches off needle together.

Worked over 2 stitches:
Row 1 (right side): tw2.
Row 2: purl.
Repeat the 2 rows.

diamond panel
The following stitches form part of the diamond panel:
mb (make bobble): knit into back and front of same stitch twice, * turn, purl these 4 stitches, turn, knit these 4 stitches, repeat from * once, slip second, third, and fourth stitches over first stitch.
c5f (cross 5 front): slip next 2 stitches onto a cable needle and hold at front of work, knit 2 stitches and purl 1 stitch from left-hand needle, knit 2 stitches from cable needle.
t3b (twist 3 back): slip next stitch onto a cable needle and hold at back of work,

knit 2 stitches from left-hand needle, purl 1 stitch from cable needle.

t3f (twist 3 front): slip next 2 stitches onto a cable needle and hold at front of work, purl 1 stitch from left-hand needle, knit 2 stitches from cable needle.

Worked over 13 stitches on a background of reverse stockinette stitch:

Row 1 (right side): purl 1, mb, purl 2, c5f, purl 2, mb, purl 1.

Row 2: knit 4, purl 2, knit 1, purl 2, knit 4.

Row 3: purl 3, t3b, knit 1, t3f, purl 3.

Row 4: knit 3, purl 2, knit 1, purl 1, knit 1, purl 2, knit 3.

Row 5: purl 2, t3b, knit 1, purl 1, knit 1, t3f, purl 2.

Row 6: knit 2, purl 2, [knit 1, purl 1] twice, knit 1, purl 2, knit 2.

Row 7: purl 1, t3b, [knit 1, purl 1] twice, knit 1, t3f, purl 1.

Row 8: knit 1, purl 2, * knit 1, purl 1, repeat from * twice, knit 1, purl 2, knit 1.

Row 9: t3b, * knit 1, purl 1, repeat from * twice, knit 1, t3f.

Row 10: purl 2, * knit 1, purl 1, repeat from * three times, knit 1, purl 2.

Row 11: t3f, * purl 1, knit 1, repeat from * twice, purl 1, t3b.

Row 12: as row 8.

Row 13: purl 1, t3f, [purl 1, knit 1] twice, purl 1, t3b, purl 1.

Row 14: as row 6.

Row 15: purl 2, t3f, purl 1, knit 1, purl 1, t3b, purl 2.

Row 16: as row 4.

Row 17: purl 3, t3f, purl 1, t3b, purl 3.

Row 18: as row 2.

Repeat these 18 rows.

fat cable

Worked over 22 stitches on a background of reverse stockinette stitch:

c8b, c8f (cable 8 back, cable 8 front): slip next 4 stitches onto a cable needle and hold at back or front of work, knit 4 stitches from left-hand needle then 4 stitches from cable needle.

Row 1 (right side): purl 3, knit 16, purl 3.

Row 2: knit 3, purl 16, knit 3.

Row 3: purl 3, c8b, c8f, purl 3.

Row 4: knit 3, purl 16, knit 3.

Rows 5–12: repeat rows 1–2 four times. Repeat these 12 rows.

making the left outer side panel (A)

With size 10½ needles, cast on 58 stitches and work in rib as follows:

Row 1 (right side): * knit 3, purl 2, repeat from * to last 3 stitches, knit 3.

Row 2: * purl 3, knit 2, repeat from * to last 3 stitches, purl 3.

Repeat these 2 rows until piece measures 5 inches ending with wrong side row.

Change to seed stitch and increase 1 stitch at beginning of every 12th row to 65 stitches. (Mark first increase with a colored thread, as all increases must be on the same side.)

Continue in seed stitch until piece measures 22½ inches from cast-on edge, ending with right side row.

Shape top: bind off 9 stitches at beginning of next and every alternate row until 11 stitches remain. Bind off.

making the right outer side panel (B)

Work as given for the left outer side panel (A) but reverse all shaping.

making the right back panel (C)

With size 10½ needles, cast on 53 stitches and work 5 inches in rib as on left outer side panel, ending with wrong side row.

The back panels have a 2-stitch garter stitch border at center back edge, which starts after the rib.

Next row: change to seed stitch,

working 2 stitches in garter stitch at end of row [center back].

Continue as established until piece measures 25½ inches from cast-on edge, ending with wrong side row.

Shape top: bind off 7 stitches at beginning of next and every alternate row until 11 stitches remain. Bind off.

making the left back panel (D)

Work as given for right back panel (C) but reverse all shaping. Remember to work the garter stitch border at beginning of first row [center back].

making the left inner side panel (E)

With size 10½ needles, cast on 62 stitches and work in raspberry stitch, increasing 1 stitch at beginning of every 5th row to 75 stitches. (Mark first increase with a colored thread, as all increases must be on the same side. Also, when increasing in raspberry stitch, make a new bobble only when you have increased 4 stitches, not before, or you will have too many stitches on the needle.)

Continue without shaping until knitting measures 17 inches, ending with right side row.

Shape top: bind off 11 stitches on next and every alternate row until 9 stitches remain. Bind off.

making the right inner side panel (F)

Work as given for the left inner side panel (E) but reverse all shaping.

making the center back panel (G)

With size 10½ needles, cast on 78 stitches and work the Aran pattern as follows:

Row 1 (right side): purl 7; work 64 stitch Aran pattern as follows—tw2, purl 2, 13 stitches from diamond panel, purl 2, tw2, 22 stitches from fat cable, tw2, purl 2, 13 stitches from diamond panel, purl 2, tw2; purl 7.

Row 2: knit 7, work row 2 of Aran pattern, knit 7.

Increase 1 stitch at each end of every 16th row until 86 stitches on needle, and then increase at each end of every 3rd row until 100 stitches on needle, and making bobbles (mb) at center of extra stitches on every row 1 of diamond panel (see photograph). (All increased stitches are worked in reverse stockinette stitch.) Continue without shaping until piece measures 19 inches.

Shape top: decrease 1 stitch at each end of next 15 rows. *70 stitches.* Bind off 2 stitches at beginning of next 9 rows. *52 stitches.* Bind off.

making the front panel, including arm fronts (H)

With size 10½ needles, cast on 118 stitches and work 5 inches in rib. Referring to the photograph, now work in pattern as follows:

Next row: work 22 stitches from fat cable, purl 5, work 64 stitches from Aran pattern as on center back panel (G), purl 5, work 22 stitches from fat cable. This sets the pattern. Continue in pattern until piece measures 12 inches from cast-on edge, ending with wrong side row.

Work across first 22 stitches (fat cable) and place on stitch holder or spare yarn, work across next 74 stitches, place last 22 stitches on stitch holder or spare yarn. Continue on 74 stitches in pattern until piece measures 14½ inches from beginning.

Work in reverse stockinette stitch, decreasing 1 stitch at each end of 1st and every 6th row until 68 stitches remain. Continue without shaping until reverse stockinette stitch measures 10 inches.

Shape top: decrease 1 stitch at each end of next and every 4th row until 62 stitches remain.

Decrease 1 stitch at each end of every 3rd row to 56 stitches, on every alternate row to 44 stitches and finally on every row until 32 stitches remain. Bind off. Return to first set of stitches on stitch holder. With wrong side facing, rejoin yarn. Remembering which row of the fat cable you are on, continue without shaping until piece measures 14½ inches (24¼ inches from cast-on edge).

Shape top: decrease 1 stitch at each end of next and every alternate row until 16 stitches remain. Bind off.

With right side of work facing, return to last set of stitches on stitch holder. Rejoin yarn and complete to match first side. Bind off.

making the cushion top, including the front gusset (I)

With size 10½ needles, cast on 70 stitches and work in pattern as follows:

Row 1: purl 3, work 64 stitches from Aran pattern, purl 3.

This sets the pattern. Continue in pattern without shaping until piece measures 16½ inches. (Place a colored thread at each end of the row after the first 4 inches —this marks the "fold line" for the front of the cushion as it is part of the gusset).

Shape cushion: decrease 1 stitch each end of next and every 4th row until 64 stitches remain.

Decrease 1 stitch at each end of every 3rd row to 58 stitches, on every alternate row until 46 stitches remain and finally every row until 32 stitches remain. Bind off.

making the cushion base (J)

Work as given for the cushion top

but continue until piece measures 12½ inches before shaping the cushion.

making the cushion gusset (K)

Cast on 15 stitches and work 54 inches in seed stitch. Bind off.

making up the armchair cover

Weave in any loose ends. Working on a large flat surface, pin the pieces out carefully. Gently steam each piece, taking care not to flatten the stitch patterns.

Join A (left outer side panel) to C (right back panel) and B (right outer side panel) to D (left back panel).

Join E (left inner side panel) to G (center back panel) and F (right inner side panel) to G (center back panel).

Join the inner panels E (left inner side panel), G (center back panel), and F (right inner side panel) to the outer panels A, C, D, and B along the top edge of the chair.

Attach H (front panel), starting at the rib and working around to the front of each arm.

Finally sew in J (cushion base), pinning and easing as you go.

Sew on four pairs of tapes to the garter stitch back opening as shown.

finishing the cushion

Attach K (gusset) to I (cushion top) first. Fold cushion along the line of colored threads and attach K (gusset). Pin carefully, then stitch.

Attach J (cushion base), leaving an opening to insert the cushion pad, then sew opening.

beaded and sequined muffler

This simple but highly effective little neck scarf is made from an assortment of natural-colored yarns—linen, cotton, chenille, silk, and tweed—joined in at random. No real formal plan or instructions are necessary for this scarf; the key is to select a group of yarns with colors and textures that personally inspire you, then add them in as you like. You may choose to select more vibrant colors to work with a favorite coat, or you may wish to recycle yarns from faithful old sweaters (see page 26). The finished scarf is strewn with wooden beads and iridescent sequins, sewn into position, to assure a very unique accessory.

making the
beaded and
sequined muffler

materials

Assorted yarns from your stash, all
approximately light worsted or DK in
weight. Use one strand, or two or three
strands of your chosen yarns plied
together, to achieve the correct weight
and gauge (see page 25). The following
yarns were used to make the muffler
shown here:

    Rowan *Linen Drape*
    Rowan *DK Cotton*
    Rowan *Wool Cotton*
    Rowan *Chenille*
    Rowan *Summer Tweed*

1 pair of size 6 (4mm) knitting needles, or
    size appropriate for your chosen yarns
Approximately 100 iridescent sequins
Approximately 100 flat-cut wooden beads
Large sewing needle
Cotton sewing thread

size

One size (approximately 40 inches by
8¾ inches)

gauge

18 stitches and 22 rows = 4 inches/10cm
in stockinette stitch using size 6 needles.
Always work a gauge swatch and change
needles accordingly if necessary.

tips

When working in stockinette stitch,
slipping the first stitch and knitting
the last stitch of each row will give a
neat finish that will stop the edges
from rolling.

knitting the muffler

With size 6 needles and your chosen yarn, cast on 34 stitches.

Work in garter stitch—knit every row—joining in, breaking off, and joining in different yarns at random until piece measures 9 inches. (When changing yarns in the middle of a row, drop the yarn no longer required to the wrong side of the work and join the new yarn, twisting the ends of each together to avoid a hole. These ends can be stranded across the wrong side of the work for a few stitches as you work or can be sewn in during finishing.)

Next row: decrease 4 stitches evenly across next row. *30 stitches.*
Change to stockinette stitch, continuing to join in new yarns at random, until knitting measures 31½ inches.

Next row: increase 4 stitches evenly across next row. *34 stitches.*
Change to garter stitch, continuing to join in new yarns at random, until knitting measures 40 inches. Bind off.

finishing the muffler

Working on a flat surface, lay the muffler out carefully.
Gently steam, taking care not to flatten the stitch patterns.
Scatter the beads and sequins over the garter-stitch borders.
Using cotton sewing thread, sew the beads and sequins in place either individually or using long stitches across the wrong side of the muffler.

denim beanbag

A new twist on jeans with a sweater! Not to wear this time, though,
but to sit on. Denim jeans have always been considered more desirable
once faded, worn, patched, and recycled. Just like its woven cousin,
denim yarn shrinks and fades to a wonderful color after washing.
This beanbag uses both the jeans and the yarn in its construction;
patched pieces of jeans are sewn together with ribbed knit pieces.
The beanbag is made from six lozenge-shape pieces, three in denim
knit and three in denim fabric, which are sewn into a large hexagon
of fabric for the bottom opening and a smaller hexagon of denim
knit for the top. The detailing is the most interesting to do; try to
incorporate pockets, buttons, and seams into your design to create
a relaxed, casual, and fun piece of furniture.

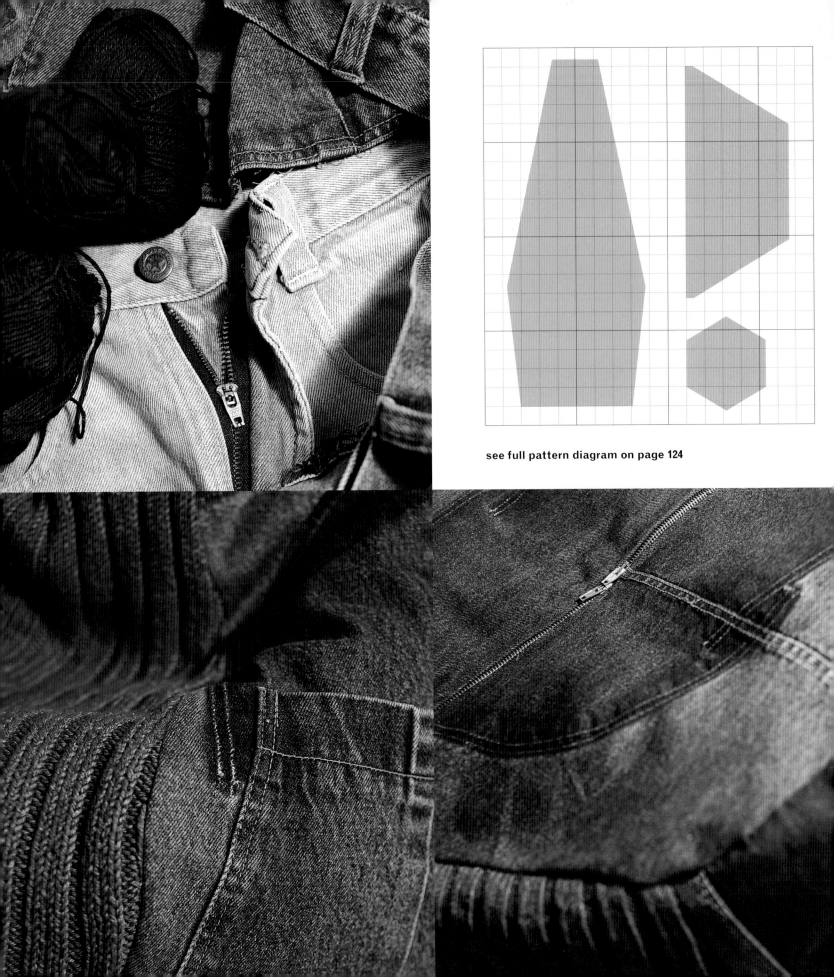

see full pattern diagram on page 124

making the denim beanbag

materials

11 1¾-ounce (50-gram) balls Rowan *Denim*

1 pair of size 5 (3.75mm) knitting needles

1 pair of size 6 (4mm) knitting needles

1 or 2 pairs of old jeans

Approximately 2¼ yards calico fabric

Polystyrene beads

1 x 16-inch or 2 x 8-inch jean zipper
  or Velcro

size

One size (beanbag measures approximately 32¼ inches by 89½ inches)

gauge

20 stitches and 24 rows = 4 inches/10cm in stockinette stitch using size 6 needles before washing and blocking. Always work a gauge swatch and change needles accordingly if necessary. Once you have worked your swatch, wash and dry it as per the instructions on the yarn label. Measure the swatch again—you should now have a gauge of 20 stitches and 30 rows to 4 inches square. (The swatch should shrink approximately 20 percent in length.) The instructions given allow for the shrinkage of the knitted panels only.

tips

Keep the patched denim simple, but incorporate pockets, buttons, and seams for extra detail and practicality. If insufficient, patch in another piece to size and cut all to shape. A ½-inch seam allowance is included in the pattern pieces.

making the side panels (work 3 pieces)

With size 6 needles, cast on 60 stitches. **Row 1 (right side):** * knit 3, purl 2, repeat from * to end. **Row 2:** * knit 2, purl 3, repeat from * to end. These 2 rows form the rib. Work an additional 6 rows in rib. Increase 1 stitch at each end of next and every 9th row to 80 stitches, working additional stitches into knit 3, purl 2 rib. Work 3 rows in rib. Decrease 1 stitch at each end of next and every 6th row until 24 stitches remain. Bind off.

making the top panel

With size 5 needles, cast on 24 stitches. Work 2 rows in stockinette stitch. Increase 1 stitch at each end of next and every 3rd row to 48 stitches. Work 2 rows in stockinette stitch. Decrease 1 stitch at each end of next and every 3rd row until 24 stitches remain. Bind off.

Weave in all the yarn ends. Launder the knitted panels as per the instructions on the yarn label. Lay panels out flat and press into shape.

cutting the denim patches

Using the templates on page 124, draw out pattern pieces on newspaper or brown paper. Cut 3 large lozenge panels and 2 half hexagons from the denim jeans. Use a strip from the waistband to make a carry handle.

stitching the beanbag

Sew short top sides of lozenge panels to knitted hexagon, alternating knitted and denim panels. Double-stitch for extra strength. Sew two half hexagons together, turning seam allowance in at center and inserting either one long 16-inch zipper or two 8-inch zippers (with pulls towards the center). Alternatively,

use Velcro instead to fasten the beanbag.

making the calico liner

Using the same templates on page 124, cut 6 large lozenge panels, 2 half hexagon shapes, and 1 small hexagon shape from the calico. Sew short top sides of lozenge panels to sides of small hexagon, with ½-inch seams. Join all side seams of lozenge panels. Sew two half hexagon pieces to bottom edges of lozenge panels, leaving center edges open but overlapping.

filling the beanbag

Insert the calico liner into the finished beanbag, attaching the liner to the inside of the beanbag at the top with a few secure stitches. Carefully fill the liner with beads. Sew the slit at the bottom of the liner to close. Zip up the denim bag. Squish into shape and relax.

hanging basket liner

Cotton kitchen twine is strong, cheap, and readily available. Of course, it is wonderfully natural and biodegradable as well, which makes it ideal around the garden. Here it is knit to create a simple, yet effective and functional, hanging basket liner for use inside or out. The liner, worked in simple stockinette stitch on two needles, has an edge of garter stitch slightly taller than the basket to allow for condensing once filled with earth. It is decorated further with a twine pompom. Plant with vibrant seasonal flowers, architectural grasses, or striking euphorbia, and you've got an ideal chic and economical gift for a keen gardener.

making the hanging basket liner

materials
2 93-yard balls natural-colored medium
  cotton kitchen twine
1 size 6 (4mm) circular knitting needle,
  16 inches (40cm) long
1 size 7 (4.5mm) circular knitting needle,
  16 inches (40cm) long
Large sewing needle
Cardboard
Scissors

size
One size (approximately 16 inches in diameter)

gauge
16 stitches and 21 rows = 4 inches/10cm in stockinette stitch using size 7 needles.
Always work a gauge swatch and change needles accordingly if necessary.

tips
Use circular knitting needles to work a tubular piece. After casting on, when you join
the ends to knit the first round, make sure that the stitches are not twisted around the
needle and are evenly distributed. A twisted cast-on cannot be rectified once you have
worked a round. To keep the stitches untwisted, keep the cast-on edge facing the
center, or work one row before joining the stitches, then sew the gap closed later.
To identify the beginning of each new round, place a colored thread between the first
and last cast-on stitches before joining. Repeat for each subsequent round.

knitting the liner

With a size 6 circular needle, cast on 128 stitches.

Row 1: knit 1 round

Row 2: purl 1 round.

Repeat the last two rows twice.

Change to a size 7 circular needle and knit 12 rounds.

Next row: (knit 6 stitches, knit 2 together) to end. *112 stitches.*

Knit 7 rounds.

Next row: (knit 5 stitches, knit 2 together) to end. *96 stitches.*

Knit 3 rounds.

Next row: (knit 4 stitches, knit 2 together) to end. *80 stitches.*

Knit 3 rounds.

Next row: (knit 3 stitches, knit 2 together) to end. *64 stitches.*

Knit 3 rounds.

Next row: (knit 2 stitches, knit 2 together) to end. *48 stitches.*

Knit 3 rounds.

Next row: (knit 1 stitch, knit 2 together) to end. *32 stitches.*

Knit 3 rounds.

Next row: (knit 2 together) to end. *16 stitches.*

Knit 3 rounds.

Next row: (knit 2 together) to end. *8 stitches.*

Knit 1 round.

finishing the liner

Cut the twine and thread through the remaining stitches, pull tightly to gather and secure.

making the pompom

Cut 2 cardboard circles 2¾ inches in diameter. Cut a hole in the center of each circle. Wind the twine into a ball small enough to pass through the center hole. Holding the 2 circles together, wind the twine round and round, keeping the strands close together. Work as many layers as possible before center hole becomes too small for the twine to pass through. Using sharp scissors, slip a blade between the layers of cardboard and cut around the circumference of the circle. Slip a length of twine between the layers and around the center of the pompom. Pull tight and knot the twine, now cut away the card. Shake, fluff up, and trim the pompom to shape. Attach to a length of twine and sew in position at center of liner.

planting

Mold the liner a little with your hands, pulling into position. Place in a wire basket or planter of your choice. Fill the container with soil mixture and plant with your favorite blooms or seeds.

gardener's kneeler

Here is a firm and functional cushion to kneel on in the garden when doing the weeding or tending to plants. The top is knitted in simple cotton kitchen twine, which is matte in finish and gives strong stitch clarity. It is then embroidered with a simple running stitch in natural leather thonging for decorative detail. Natural color burlap is recycled to make a practical and durable backing; a coated sacking in a vibrant color would make a durable alternative. The firm filling is provided by a piece of foam rubber cut to shape and tied in with natural cotton webbing tapes. Alternatively, make a square cushion with a softer filling for use on a chair in the greenhouse or potting shed or on a porch.

making the gardener's kneeler

materials
3 93-yard balls natural-colored medium
  cotton kitchen twine
1 pair of size 9 (5.5mm) knitting needles
Approximately 3¼ yards leather thonging
Blunt-ended needle
Approximately ¾ yard burlap (from a bag,
  if possible), sacking, or fabric of your
  choice for backing
Cotton tape for ties
Large sewing needle
High-density foam rubber, cut to shape
  and mitered (available from most
  fabric stores)

size
One size (kneeler measures approximately 20 inches by 11 inches)

gauge
13 stitches and 18 rows = 4 inches/10cm in stockinette stitch using size 9 needles.
Always work a gauge swatch and change needles accordingly if necessary.

knitting the top

With size 9 needles, cast on 65 stitches. Work in stockinette stitch until piece measures 11 inches. Bind off.

finishing the top

Weave in all the yarn ends and block to shape with a steam iron.

Using the large sewing needle and leather thonging, embroider neat running stitches all around the edge of the top by working 4 stitches in and 4 rows in, placing embroidery stitch in every alternate knit stitch. Finish with a knot on the inside.

making the backing

Cut the fabric to the same size as the knitted top plus 1 inch extra all around for the seam allowance. If using burlap, utilize the sewn edges of the original bag, and you may wish to incorporate any authentic markings for extra detail. Turn 1 inch to the wrong side around the edge of the backing, then with wrong sides together, sew the knitted top to the backing around two long sides and one short side with fine running stitches or blanket stitches. Sew lengths of cotton tape to either side of the opening, placing the ties approximately 3 inches from the sides.

Insert foam rubber and tie bows to close opening.

58 59
56 57
54 55
52 53
50 51
48 49
46 47
44 45
42 43
40 41
38 39
36 37
34 35
32 33
30 31
28 29
26 27
24 25
22 23
20 21
18 19
16 17
14 15
12 13
10 11
8 9
6 7
4 5
2 3
1

A
B
C
D

rose chintz cushion

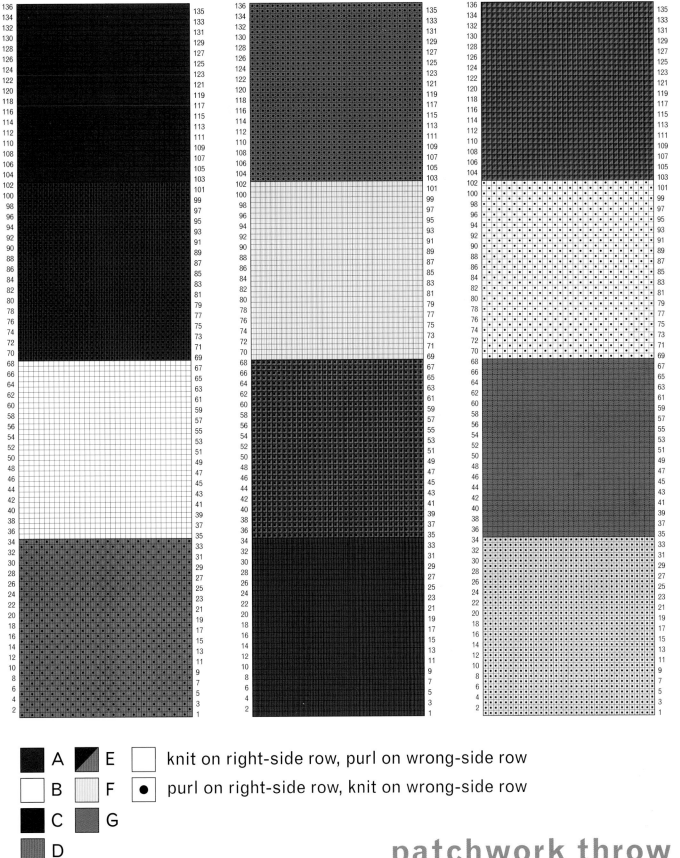

A ▨ E ☐ knit on right-side row, purl on wrong-side row

B ☐ F ● purl on right-side row, knit on wrong-side row

C

D G

patchwork throw

flower

  A

B

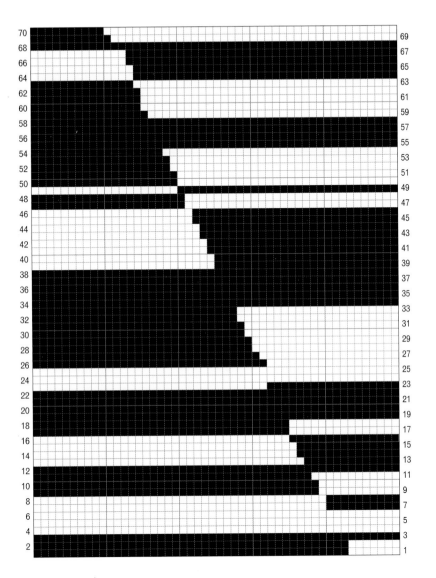

stripes

blocks

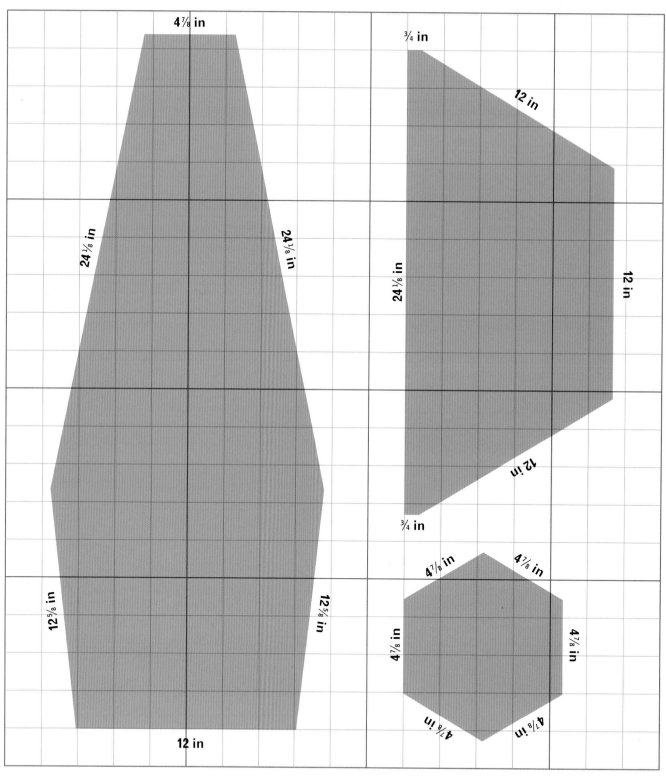

4⅞ in

¾ in

12 in

24⅛ in

24⅛ in

24⅛ in

12 in

12 in

¾ in

12⅝ in

12⅝ in

4⅞ in

4⅞ in

4⅞ in

4⅞ in

4⅞ in

4⅞ in

12 in

one square = 2 inches

denim beanbag

substituting yarns

Although I have recommended a specific yarn for many of the projects in the book, you can substitute others.

If you decide to use an alternative yarn, any other brand of yarn that is of the same weight and type should serve as well, but to avoid disappointing results, it is very important that you test the yarn first.

Purchase a substitute yarn that is as close as possible to the original in thickness, weight, and texture so that it will be compatible with the instructions. Buy only one ball to start with, so you can try out the effect. Calculate the number of balls you will need by yardage/meterage rather than by weight. The recommended knitting-needle size and knitting gauge on the yarn labels are extra guides to the yarn thickness.

other yarns

Metallic wire is available in craft stores or from wire merchants, such as:
Metalliferous
34 West 64th St, New York, NY 10036
Tel: 212-944-0909 www.metalliferous.com

Kitchen twine comes in various thicknesses and is not always labeled with an exact amount, so you may need to experiment with a single ball to start with. The Hanging Basket Liner (pages 112–115) and the Gardener's Kneeler (pages 116–119) are made with natural-colored medium kitchen twine, which is available from hardware stores.

Leather thonging is available in craft stores or from leather merchants/saddlery shops.

yarn suppliers

To obtain Rowan yarns, look below to find a distributor or store in your area.
www.knitrowan.com

Sirdar yarn is available from:
Knitting Fever Inc.
35 Debevoise Ave.
Roosevelt, NY 11575
Tel: 516-546-3600 www.knittingfever.com

Rowan Stockists/United States

DISTRIBUTOR: Westminster Fibers,
4 Townsend West, Suite 8, Nashua, NH 03064.
Tel: (603) 886-5041/5043
e-mail: wfibers@aol.com

ALABAMA
HUNTSVILLE: Yarn Expressions,
7914 S Memorial Parkway, Huntsville, AL 35802.
Tel: (256) 881-0260 www.yarnexpressions.com
ARIZONA
TUCSON: Purls, 7862 North Oracle Rd.,
Tucson, AZ 85704. Tel: (520) 797-8118.
ARKANSAS
LITTLE ROCK: The Handworks Gallery,
2911 Kavanaugh Blvd., Little Rock, AR 72205.
Tel: (501) 664-6300 ww.handworksgallery.com
CALIFORNIA
ANAHEIM HILLS: Velona Needlecraft,
5701-M Santa Ana Canyon Rd., Anaheim
Hills, CA 92807. Tel: (714) 974-1570
www.velona.com
CARMEL: Knitting by the Sea, 5th & Junipero,
Carmel, CA 93921. Tel: (800) 823-3189
BERKELEY: eKnitting.com,
Tel: (800) 392-6494 www.eKnitting.com
LA JOLLA: Knitting in La Jolla,
7863 Girard Ave., La Jolla, CA 92037.
Tel: (800) 956-5648.
LONG BEACH: Alamitos Bay Yarn Co.,
174 Marina Dr., Long Beach, CA 90803.
Tel: (562) 799-8484 www.yarncompany.com
LAFAYETTE: Big Sky Studio,
961 C Moraga Rd., Lafayette, CA 94549.

Tel: (925) 284-1020 www.bigskystudio.com
LOS ALTOS: Uncommon Threads,
293 State St., Los Altos, CA 94022.
Tel: (650) 941-1815
MENDOCINO: Mendocino Yarn,
45066 Ukiah St., Mendocino, CA 95460.
Tel: (888) 530-1400
www.mendocinoyarnshop.com
OAKLAND: The Knitting Basket,
2054 Mountain Blvd., Oakland, CA 94611.
Tel: (800) 654-4887 www.theknittingbasket.com
REDONDO BEACH: L'Atelier,
17141–2 Catalina, Redondo Beach, CA 90277.
Tel: (310) 540-4440
ROCKLIN: Filati Yarns, 4810 Granite Dr., Suite
A-7, Rocklin, CA 95677. Tel: (800) 398-9043
SAN FRANCISCO: Greenwich Yarns,
2073 Greenwich St., San Francisco, CA 94123.
Tel: (415) 567-2535
www.greenwichyarn.citysearch.com
SANTA BARBARA: In Stitches,
5 E Figueroa, Santa Barbara, CA 93101.
Tel: (805) 962-9343 www.institchesyarns.com
SANTA MONICA: L'Atelier on Montana,
1202 Montana Ave., Santa Monica, CA 90403.
Tel: (310) 394-4665
Wild Fiber, 1453 E 14th St., Santa Monica,
CA 90404. Tel: (310) 458-2748
STUDIO CITY: La Knitterie Parisienne,
12642-44 Ventura Blvd., Studio City, CA 91604.
Tel: (818) 766-1515
THOUSAND OAKS: Eva's Needleworks,
1321 E Thousand Oaks Blvd., Thousand Oaks,
CA 91360. Tel: (803) 379-0722
COLORADO
COLORADO SPRINGS: Needleworks by
Holly Berry, 2409 W Colorado Ave., CO 80904.
Tel: (719) 636-1002
DENVER: Strawberry Tree, 2200 S Monaco
Parkway, Denver, CO 80222. Tel: (303) 759-4244
LAKEWOOD: Showers of Flowers,
6900 W Colfax Ave., Lakewood, CO 80215.
Tel: (303) 233-2525
www.showersofflowers.com
LONGMONT: Over the Moon, 600 S Airport
Rd., Bldg A, Ste D, Longmont, CO 80503.
Tel: (303) 485-6778 www.over-the-moon.com

CONNECTICUT

AVON: The Wool Connection, 34 E Main St., Avon, CT 06001. Tel: (860) 678-1710 www.woolconnection.com

DEEP RIVER: Yarns Down Under, 37C Hillside Terrace, Deep River, CT 06417. Tel: (860) 526-9986 www.yarnsdownunder.com

MYSTIC: Mystic River Yarns, 14 Holmes St., Mystic, CT 06355. Tel: (860) 536-4305

SOUTHBURY: Selma's Yarn & Needleworks, 450 Heritage Rd., Southbury, CT 06488. Tel: (203) 264-4838 www.selmasyarns.com

WESTPORT: Hook 'N' Needle, 1869 Post Rd., E Westport, CT 06880. Tel: (203) 259-5119 www.hook-n-needle.com

WOODBRIDGE: The Yarn Barn, 24 Selden St., Woodbridge, CT 06525. Tel: (203) 389-5117 www.theyarnbarn.com

GEORGIA

ATLANTA: Strings & Strands, 4632 Wieuca Rd., Atlanta, GA 30342. Tel: (404) 252-9662.

ILLINOIS

CLARENDON HILLS: Flying Colors Inc., 15 Walker Ave., Clarendon Hills, IL 60514. Tel: (630) 325-0888

CHICAGO: Weaving Workshop, 2218 N Lincoln Ave., Chicago, IL 60614. Tel: (773) 929-5776

OAK PARK: Tangled Web Fibers, 177 S Oak Park Rd., Oak Park, IL 60302. Tel: (708) 445-8335 www.tangledwebfibers.com

NORTHBROOK: Three Bags Full, 1856 Walters Ave., Northbrook, IL 60062. Tel: (847) 291-9933

ST. CHARLES: The Fine Line Creative Arts Center, 6 N 158 Crane Rd., St. Charles, IL 60175. Tel: (630) 584-9443

SPRINGFIELD: Nancy's Knitworks, 1650 W Wabash Ave., Springfield, IL 62704. Tel: (217) 546-0600

INDIANA

FORT WAYNE: Cass St. Depot, 1044 Cass St., Fort Wayne, IN 46802. Tel: (219) 420-2277 www.cassstreetdepot.com

INDIANAPOLIS: Mass Ave. Knit Shop, 521 E North St., Indianapolis, IN 46204. Tel: (800) 675-8565

KANSAS

ANDOVER: Whimsies, 307 N Andover Rd., Andover, KS 67002. Tel: (316) 733-8881

LAWRENCE: The Yarn Barn, 930 Mass Ave., Lawrence, KS 66044. Tel: (800) 468-0035

KENTUCKY

LOUISVILLE: Handknitters Limited, 11726 Main St., Louisville, KY 40243. Tel: (502) 254-9276 www.handknittersltd.com

MAINE

CAMDEN: Stitchery Square, 11 Elm St., Camden, ME 04843. Tel: (207) 236-9773 www.stitching.com/stitcherysquare

FREEPORT: Grace Robinson & Co., 208 US Route 1, Suite 1, Freeport, ME 04032. Tel: (207) 865 6110

HANCOCK: Shirley's Yarn & Crafts, Route 1, Hancock, ME 04640. Tel: (207) 667-7158

MARYLAND

ANNAPOLIS: Yarn Garden, 2303 I Forest Dr., Annapolis, MD 21401. Tel: (410) 224-2033

BALTIMORE: Woolworks, 6305 Falls Rd., Baltimore, MD 21209. Tel: (410) 337-9030

BETHESDA: The Needlework Loft, 4706 Bethesda Ave., Bethesda, MD. Tel: (301) 652-8688

Yarns International, 5110 Ridgefield Rd., Bethesda, MD 20816. Tel: (301) 913-2980.

GLYNDON: Woolstock, 4848 Butler Rd., Glyndon, MD 21071. Tel: (410) 517-1020

MASSACHUSETTS

BROOKLINE VILLAGE: A Good Yarn, 4 Station St., Brookline Village, MA 02447. Tel: (617) 731-4900 www.agoodyarnonline.com

CAMBRIDGE: Woolcott & Co, 61 JFK St., Cambridge, MA 02138-4931. Tel: (617) 547-2837

DENNIS: Ladybug Knitting Shop, 612 Route 6, Dennis, MA 02638. Tel: (508) 385-2662 www.ladybugknitting.com

DUXBURY: The Wool Basket, 19 Depot St., Duxbury, MA 02332 Tel: (781) 934-2700

HARVARD: The Fiber Loft, 9 Massachusetts Ave., Harvard, MA 01451. Tel: (800) 874-9276

LENOX: Colorful Stitches, 48 Main St., Lenox, MA 01240. Tel: (800) 413-6111 www.colorful-stitches.com

LEXINGTON: Wild & Woolly Studio, 7A Meriam St., Lexington, MA 02173. Tel: (781) 861-7717

MILTON: Snow Goose, 10 Bassett St., Milton Market Place, Milton, MA 02186. Tel: (617) 698-1190

NORTHAMPTON: Northampton Wools, 11 Pleasant St., Northampton, MA 01060. Tel: (413) 586-4331

WORCESTER: Knit Latte, 1062 Pleasant St., Worcester, MA 01602. Tel: (508) 754-6300

MICHIGAN

BIRMINGHAM: Knitting Room, 251 Merrill, Birmingham, MI 48009. Tel: (248) 540-3623 www.knittingroom.com

GRAND HAVEN: The Fibre House, 117 Washington St., Grand Haven, MI 49417. Tel: (616) 844-2497 www.forknitters.com

TRAVERSE CITY: Lost Art Yarn Shoppe, 123 E Front St., Traverse City, MI 49684. Tel: (231) 941-1263

WYOMING: Threadbender Yarn Shop, 2767 44th St. SW, Wyoming, MI 49509. Tel: (888) 531-6642

YPSILANTE: Knit A Round Yarn Shop, 2888 Washtinaw Ave., Ypsilante, MI 48197. Tel: (734) 528-5648

MINNESOTA

MINNEAPOLIS: Linden Hills Yarn, 2720 W 43rd St., Minneapolis, MN 55410. Tel: (612) 929-1255

Needleworks Unlimited, 3006 W 50th St., Minneapolis, MN 55410. Tel: (612) 925-2454

MINNETONKA: Skeins, 11309 Highway 7, Minnetonka, MN 55305. Tel: (952) 939-4166

ST. PAUL: The Yarnery KMK Crafts, 840 Grand Ave., St. Paul, MN 55105. Tel: (651) 222-5793

WHITE BEAR LAKE: A Sheepy Yarn Shoppe, 2185 3rd St., White Bear Lake, MN 55110. Tel: (800) 480-5462

MONTANA

STEVENSVILLE: Wild West Wools, 3920 Suite B Highway 93N, Stevensville, MT 59870. Tel: (406) 777-4114

NEBRASKA

OMAHA: Personal Threads Boutique, 8025 W Dodge Rd., Omaha, NE 68114. Tel: (402) 391-7733 www.personalthreads.com

NEW HAMPSHIRE
CONCORD: Elegant Ewe, 71 S Main St.,
Concord, NH 03301. Tel: (603) 226-0066
EXETER: Charlotte's Web,
Exeter Village Shops, 137 Epping Rd., Route
27, Exeter, NH 03833. Tel: (888) 244-6460
NASHUA: Rowan USA, 4 Townsend West,
Nashua, NH. Tel: (603) 886-5041/5043

NEW JERSEY
CHATHAM: Stitching Bee,
240A Main St., Chatham, NJ 07928.
Tel: (973) 635-6691 www.thestitchingbee.com
HOBOKEN: Hoboken Handknits,
671 Willow Ave., Hoboken, NJ 07030.
Tel: (201) 653-2545
LAMBERTVILLE: Simply Knit,
23 Church St., Lambertville, NJ 08530.
Tel: (609) 397-7101
PRINCETON: Glenmarle Woolworks,
301 North Harrison St., Princeton, NJ 08540.
Tel: (609) 921-3022

NEW MEXICO
ALBUQUERQUE: Village Wools,
3801 San Mateo Ave. NE, Albuquerque,
NM 87110. Tel: (505) 883-2919
SANTA FE: Needle's Eye,
839 Paseo de Peralta, Santa Fe, NM 87501.
Tel: (505) 982-0706

NEW YORK
BEDFORD HILLS: Lee's Yarn Center,
733 N Bedford Rd., Bedford Hills, NY 10507.
Tel: (914) 244-3400 www.leesyarn.com
BUFFALO: Elmwood Yarn Shop,
1639 Hertel Ave., Buffalo, NY 14216.
Tel: (716) 834-7580
GARDEN CITY: Garden City Stitches,
725 Franklin Ave., Garden City, NY 11530. Tel:
(516) 739-5648 www.gardencitystitches.com
HUNTINGTON: Knitting Corner, 718 New York
Ave., Huntington, NY 11743. Tel: (631) 421-2660
ITHACA: The Homespun Boutique,
314 E State St., Ithaca, NY 14850.
Tel: (607) 277-0954
MIDDLETOWN: Bonnie's Cozy Knits.
Tel: (845) 344-0229
NEW YORK CITY: Downtown Yarns,
45 Ave. A, New York, NY 10009.
Tel: (212) 995-5991

Lion & The Lamb, 1460 Lexington Ave.,
New York, NY 10128. Tel: (212) 876-4303
Purl, 137 Sullivan St., New York, NY 10012.
Tel: (212) 420-8796 www.purlsoho.com
The Yarn Company, 2274 Broadway,
New York, NY 10024. Tel: (212) 787-7878
Yarn Connection, 218 Madison Ave.,
New York, NY 10016. Tel: (212) 684-5099
Woolgathering, 318 E 84th St., New York, NY
10028. Tel: (212) 734-4747
SKANEATELES: Elegant Needles, 7 Jordan St.,
Skaneateles, NY 13152. Tel: (315) 685-9276

NORTH CAROLINA
GREENSBORO: Yarn Etc., 231 S Elm St.,
Greensboro, NC 27401. Tel: (336) 370-1233
RALEIGH: Great Yarns, 1208 Ridge Rd.,
Raleigh, NC. Tel: (919) 832-3599
WILSON: Knit Wit, 1-B Ward Blvd. N, Wilson,
NC 27893. Tel: (252) 291-8149

NORTH DAKOTA
FARGO: Yarn Renaissance,
1226 S University Dr., Fargo, ND 58103.
Tel: (701) 280-1478

OHIO
AURORA: Edie's Knit Shop,
214 Chillicothe Rd., Aurora, OH 44202.
Tel: (330) 562-7226
CINCINNATI: One More Stitch,
2030 Madison Rd., Cincinnati, OH 45208.
Tel: (513) 533-1170
Wizard Weavers, 2701 Observatory Rd.,
Cincinnati, OH 45208. Tel: (513) 871-5750
CLEVELAND: Fine Points,
12620 Larchmere Blvd., Cleveland, OH 44120.
Tel: (216) 229-6644 www.finepoints.com
COLUMBUS: Wolfe Fiber Art,
1188 W 5th Ave., Columbus, OH 43212.
Tel: (614) 487-9980

OREGON
ASHLAND: Web-sters, 11 N Main St.,
Ashland, OR 97520. Tel: (800) 482-9801
www.yarnatwebsters.com
COOS BAY: My Yarn Shop,
264 B Broadway, Coos Bay, OR 97420.
Tel: (888) 664-9276 www.myyarnshop.com
LAKE OSWEGO: Molehill Farm,
16722 SW Boones Ferry Rd., Lake Oswego,
OR 97035. Tel: (503) 697-9554

PORTLAND: Northwest Wools,
3524 SW Troy St., Portland, OR 97219.
Tel: (503) 244-5024 www.northwestwools.com
Yarn Garden, 1413 SE Hawthorne Blvd.,
Portland, OR 97214. Tel: (503) 239-7950
www.yarngarden.net

PENNSYLVANIA
KENNETT SQUARE: Wool Gathering,
131 E State St., Kennett Square, PA 19348.
Tel: (610) 444-8236
PHILADELPHIA: Sophie's Yarn,
2017 Locust St., Philadelphia, PA 19103.
Tel: (215) 977-9276
Tangled Web, 7900 Germantown Ave.,
Philadelphia, PA. Tel: (215) 242-1271
SEWICKLEY: Yarns Unlimited, 435 Beaver St.,
Sewickley, PA 15143. Tel: (412) 741-8894

RHODE ISLAND
PROVIDENCE: A Stitch Above Ltd.,
190 Wayland Ave., Providence, RI 02906.
Tel: (800) 949-5648
www.astitchaboveknitting.com
TIVERTON: Sakonnet Purls, 3988 Main Rd.,
Tiverton, RI 02878. Tel: (888) 624-9902
www.sakonnetpurls.com

SOUTH CAROLINA
AIKEN: Barbara Sue Brodie Needlepoint &
Yarn, 148 Lauren St., Aiken, SC 29801.
Tel: (803) 644-0990

TENNESSEE
NASHVILLE: Angel Hair Yarn Co.,
4121 Hillsboro Park, #205, Nashville, TN 37215.
Tel: (615) 269-8833 www.angelhairyarn.com

TEXAS
SAN ANTONIO: The Yarn Barn of San Antonio,
4300 McCullough, San Antonio, TX 78212.
Tel: (210) 826-3679

VERMONT
WOODSTOCK: The Whippletree,
7 Central St., Woodstock, VT 05091.
Tel: (802) 457-1325

VIRGINIA
CHARLOTTESVILLE: It's A Stitch Inc.,
188 Zan Rd., Charlottesville, VA 22901.
Tel: (804) 973-0331
FALLS CHURCH: Aylin's Woolgatherer, 7245
Arlington Blvd. #318, Falls Church, VA 22042.
Tel: (703) 573-1900 www.aylins-wool.com

RICHMOND: Got Yarn,
2520 Professional Rd., Richmond, VA 23235.
Tel: (888) 242-4474 www.gotyarn.com
The Knitting Basket, 5812 Grove Ave.,
Richmond, VA 23226. Tel: (804) 282-2909
WASHINGTON
BAINBRIDGE ISLAND: Churchmouse
Yarns and Teas, 118 Madrone Lane,
Bainbridge Island, WA 98110.
Tel: (206) 780-2686
BELLEVUE: Skeins! Ltd., 10635 NE 8th St.,
Suite 104, Bellevue, WA 98004.
Tel: (425) 452-1248 www.skeinslimited.com
OLYMPIA: Canvas Works, 317 N Capitol,
Olympia, WA 98501. Tel: (360) 352-4481
POULSBO: Wild & Wooly,
19020 Front St., Poulsbo, WA 98370.
Tel: (800) 743-2100 www.wildwooly.com
SEATTLE: The Weaving Works, 4717 Brooklyn
Ave., NE, Seattle, WA 98105.
Tel: (888) 524-1221 www.weavingworks.com
WISCONSIN
APPLETON: Jane's Knitting Hutch,
132 E Wisconsin Ave., Appleton, WI 54911.
Tel: (920) 954-9001
DELEVAN: Studio S Fiber Arts, W8903
Country Highway A, Delevan, WI 53115.
Tel: (608) 883-2123
ELM GROVE: The Yarn House,
940 Elm Grove Rd., Elm Grove, WI 53122.
Tel: (262) 786-5660
MADISON: The Knitting Tree Inc.,
2614 Monroe St., Madison, WI 53711.
Tel: (608) 238-0121
MILWAUKEE: Ruhama's,
420 E Silver Spring Dr., Milwaukee, WI 53217.
Tel: (414) 332-2660

Rowan Stockists/Canada

DISTRIBUTOR: Diamond Yarn,
9697 St. Laurent, Montreal, Quebec.
Tel: (514) 388-6188

ALBERTA
CALGARY: Birch Hill Yarns, 417–12445 Lake
Fraser Dr. SE, Calgary. Tel: (403) 271-4042
Gina Brown's, 17, 6624 Center Sr SE, Calgary.
Tel: (403) 255-2200
EDMONTON: Knit & Purl, 10412–124 St.,
Edmonton. Tel: (403) 482 2150
Wool Revival, 6513–112 Ave., Edmonton.
Tel: (403) 471-2749
ST. ALBERT: Burwood House, 205 Carnegie
Dr., St. Albert. Tel: (403) 459-4828
BRITISH COLUMBIA
COQUITLAM: Village Crafts,
1936 Como Lake Ave., Coquitlam.
Tel: (604) 931-6533
DUNCAN: The Loom,
Whippletree Junction, Box H, Duncan.
Tel: (250) 746-5250
PORT ALBERNI: Heartspun, 5242 Mary St.,
Port Alberni. Tel: (250) 724-2285
RICHMOND: Wool & Wicker,
120–12051 2nd Ave., Richmond.
Tel: (604) 275-1239
VICTORIA: Beehave Wool Shop,
2207 Oak Bay Ave., Victoria.
Tel: (250) 598-2272
WEST VANCOUVER: The Knit & Stitch
Shoppe, 2460a Marine Drive, West Vancouver.
Tel: (604) 922-1023
MANITOBA
WINNIPEG: Ram Wools, 1266 Fife St.,
Winnipeg. Tel: (204) 949-6868
www.gaspard.ca/ramwools.htm
NOVA SCOTIA
BAADECK: Baadeck Yarns,
16 Chebucto St., Baadeck.
Tel: (902) 295-2993
ONTARIO
ANCASTER: The Needle Emporium,
420 Wilson St. E, Ancaster. Tel: (800) 667-9167

AURORA: Knit or Knot, 14800 Yong St.
(Aurora Shopping Centre), Aurora.
Tel: (905) 713-1818
Needles & Knits, 15040 Yonge St., Aurora.
Tel: (905) 713-2066
CARLETON: Real Wool Shop,
142 Franktown Rd., Carleton.
Tel: (613) 257-2714
LONDON: Christina Tandberg,
Covent Garden Market, London.
Tel: (800) 668-7903
MYRTLE STATION: Ferguso's Knitting,
9585 Baldwin St. (Hwy 12), Ashburn.
OAKVILLE: The Wool Bin,
236 Lakeshore Rd. E, Oakville.
Tel: (905) 845-9512
OTTAWA: Wool Tyme,
#2 – 190 Colonnade Rd. S, Ottawa.
Tel: 1-(888) 241-7653 www.wool-tyme.com
Yarn Forward, 581 Bank St., Ottawa.
Tel: (877) yar-nfwd.
Your Creation, 3767 Mapleshore Dr.,
Kemptville, Ottawa. Tel: (613) 826 3261
TORONTO: Passionknit Ltd., 3467 Yonge St.,
Toronto. Tel: (416) 322-0688
Romni Wools Ltd., 658 Queen St. West,
Toronto. Tel: (416) 703-0202
Village Yarns, 4895 Dundas St. West, Toronto.
Tel: (416) 232-2361
The Wool Mill, 2170 Danorth Ave., Toronto.
Tel: (416) 696-2670
The Yarn Boutique, 1719A Bloor West, Toronto.
Tel: (416) 760-9129
STRATFORD: D&S Craft Supplies,
165 Downie St., Stratford. Tel: (519) 273-7962
QUEBEC
MONTREAL: A la Tricoteuse, 779 Rachel Est,
Montreal. Tel: (514) 527-2451
ST. LAMBERT: Saute Mouton, 20 Webster,
St. Lambert. Tel: (514) 671-1155
QUEBEC CITY: La Dauphine, 1487 Chemin
Ste-Foy, Quebec City. Tel: (418) 527-3030
SASKATCHEWAN
SASKATOON: Prairie Lily Knitting &
Weaving Shop, 7–1730 Quebec Ave.,
Saskatoon. Tel: (306) 665-2771